SpringerBriefs in Criminology

Translational Criminology

For further volumes:
http://www.springer.com/series/11178

About this Series

Has research made a difference to criminal justice practices and policies? Evidence-based crime policy is not just about rigorously generating a robust supply of rigorous research to find out "what works" in terms of justice interventions or "what explains" crime or offending. Evidence-based crime policy means that this supply should be attuned to the demand for research, and that research must be converted to meaningful forms and implemented with fidelity in order for practice to be receptive to science. But how does this actually happen?

An important concept in the field of evidence-based crime policy is translational criminology, or how, why, whether, and under what conditions research is converted to, and used, in practice. This Springer Brief series on translational criminology brings to both the academe and criminal justice world examples of how research becomes practice and policy, and whether research has made an impact. Each brief is written by top scholars and/or practitioners in the field who describe specific examples of how a body of research became practice (or didn't) and the lessons learned from the endeavor.

Geoffrey P. Alpert • Cynthia Lum

Police Pursuit Driving

Policy and Research

 Springer

Geoffrey P. Alpert
Department of Criminology
 and Criminal Justice
University of South Carolina
Columbia, SC, USA

Cynthia Lum
Department of Criminology
 Law and Society
George Mason University
Fairfax, VA, USA

Centre for Excellence in Policing
 and Security
Australian Research Council
Griffith University
Brisbane, QLD, Australia

ISSN 2194-6442   ISSN 2194-6450 (electronic)
ISBN 978-1-4939-0711-3   ISBN 978-1-4939-0712-0 (eBook)
DOI 10.1007/978-1-4939-0712-0
Springer New York Heidelberg Dordrecht London

Library of Congress Control Number: 2014933573

Springer is part of Springer Science+Business Media (www.springer.com)

Acknowledgements

The authors wish to thank the following individuals for their assistance with the contents of this brief: Kathryn Baxter, Michael Brown, Jaspreet Chahal, Andrew Clarke, George Fachner, Julie Grieco, Peter Hosking, Mathew Lyneham, Nancy Michel, Jordan Nichols, Jason Saunders, Heather Vovak, and mark Walker-Roberts.

Contents

List of Tables

Abstract

This brief examines a controversial and often-discussed law enforcement policy issue: police pursuits. The impact of legal analyses and research on pursuit policy is discussed in the context of the current environment of policing.

Chapter 1
Police Pursuits: A Complex Policy Arena

In today's world, police chases—or vehicular pursuits—are routine, daily occurrences. They usually result from an officer's attempt to stop a vehicle in order to enforce a traffic law or for other investigative purposes. Usually, these stops are uneventful; most drivers will pull over and negotiate an outcome with the officer, and the encounter will end without further incident. However, on some occasions the driver will refuse to stop or take evasive action and flee.

In such situations, the police officer must decide whether to pursue the vehicle, bearing in mind that if a driver refuses to stop, the officer then is accountable to the agency's pursuit policy, and other legal requirements established by local laws (including civil liability exposure). The officer must not only follow these rules, but also use his or her training and consider the risks and potential benefits of the pursuit. On the one hand, police should apprehend fleeing felons for public safety. On the other hand, all parties involved in a pursuit of a fleeing vehicle, including bystanders, risk injury without any assurance that the suspect will be apprehended. Because pursuits may result in injury, damages, and fatalities, they also receive high levels of scrutiny by the public and possibly other law enforcement agencies. Thus, while the dynamics of traffic stops and vehicular pursuits can be easy to describe, the concerns that they present to policing and to society are much more complex. These concerns include conflicting issues of public safety, crime control, civil liability, and public relations.

A quick Internet search of media headlines illustrates these many concerns:

- *Code Blue: Police Pursuits Cost a Life a Day*[1]
- *Car Being Pursued By Police Plows Into 6 High School Students; Driver Dies After Hitting A Tree*[2]

---

[1] http://www.jacksonfreepress.com/news/2012/apr/18/code-blue-police-pursuits-cost-a-life-a-day/ (downloaded 10/22/12).

[2] http://baltimore.cbslocal.com/2012/10/20/baltimore-police-investigating-fatal-car-accident-following-officer-pursuit/ (downloaded 10/22/12).

G.P. Alpert and C. Lum, *Police Pursuit Driving: Policy and Research*, SpringerBriefs in Criminology, DOI 10.1007/978-1-4939-0712-0_1, © The Author(s) 2014

- *High-speed chases, like one in Brockton, pose high risks*[3]
- *1 dead, 1 injured after chase, officer-involved shooting in Van Nuys*[4]
- *Motorcycle officer hurt in police chase*[5]
- *Man dies in police pursuit in SE Mo.*[6]
- *Police pursuit ends with vehicle striking house*[7]
- *Prince George's officer killed during pursuit on I-95*[8]

Beyond these media headlines are the real-world consequences of pursuits, and debates about how best to calculate their costs and benefits. Obviously, the apprehension of offenders, especially serious or violent ones, is a benefit to society. However, bringing a traffic offender to justice may be much less beneficial. Many police departments do not spend their resources to investigate minor violations and crimes but reserve them to go after the more serious criminals. However, when faced with a crime in progress, even if minor, officers are more likely to put forth great effort to apprehend the offender. Often, the offenses committed by fleeing individuals are unknown.[9] Thus, the question remains: What costs are justified to apprehend violators? Further, from an evidence-based perspective, how can research inform this calculation to both increase safety and reduce harm?

While it is difficult to obtain financial estimates of the costs of pursuits in law enforcement, a study done by the Virginia Municipal League Insurance Programs shows that the average pursuit claim costs insurance companies over $15,000.[10] But there are many cases across the United States that cost insurance companies and taxpayers millions of dollars. Recently the City of Chicago paid over $1.3 million for damages related to a short chase of a suspected drunk driver when the fleeing suspect hit an innocent motorist on Kedzie Avenue.[11] In fact, the City of Chicago has had to pay more than $5 million on a number of high-profile cases in which innocent bystanders were killed because of high-speed chases.[12] And, while financial

---

[3] http://www.enterprisenews.com/answerbook/bridgewater/x1224698518/Question-of-policy-on-police-pursuits-following-Brockton-fatal#ixzz2A1xtY1ZM (downloaded 10/22/12).

[4] http://latimesblogs.latimes.com/lanow/2012/10/1-dead-1-injured-after-police-chase-officer-involved-shooting-in-van-nuys.html (downloaded 10/22/12).

[5] http://www.myfoxdfw.com/story/19847895/motorcycle-officer-hurt-in-police-chase (downloaded 10/22/12).

[6] http://www.stltoday.com/news/state-and-regional/missouri/man-dies-in-police-pursuit-in-se-mo/article_6700befe-7f2e-5d58-8bd0-c85c1f205b04.html (downloaded 10/22/12).

[7] http://www.fox59.com/news/wxin-police-pursuit-ends-with-vehicle-striking-house-20121015,0,194290.column (downloaded 10/22/12).

[8] http://washingtonexaminer.com/prince-georges-officer-killed-during-pursuit-on-i-95/article/2505453#.UIU_8sXA8sd (downloaded 10/22/12).

[9] Most policies and training require that officers respond to what they have probable cause to believe has been committed, rather than respond to a hunch or instinct.

[10] https://www.vmlins.org/Newsletters/Law/injury.htm (downloaded 10/22/12).

[11] http://www.reuters.com/article/2012/09/10/idUS201759+10-Sep-2012+PRN20120910 (downloaded 10/22/12).

[12] http://www.costellaw.com/representative_cases.html.

costs of pursuits are extremely high, the emotional costs and impact on the police officers, victims, family, and even fleeing suspects are significantly higher.

In order to reduce these financial and emotional costs, law enforcement agencies have focused considerable attention on vehicular pursuits. Such concerns led the National Institute of Justice's Office of Science and Technology to form a Pursuits Management Task Force (PMTF) to examine police pursuits (Bayless and Osborne 1998). Later, the International Association of Chiefs of Police (IACP) created a national database to study pursuits (Nichols 2004) and released a model policy for pursuits in 2004.[13] Many agencies have written policies detailing when officers can pursue fleeing suspects (Lum and Fachner 2008). The policy trend continues to see agencies restrict, rather than expand, the reasons their officers are permitted to pursue other vehicles (Alpert et al. 2000; Lum and Fachner 2008).

Despite these restrictions on police pursuits, what brings further complexities into this arena is another trend: the use of traffic enforcement in policing to generate crime control benefits. Traffic enforcement as a law enforcement tool has taken on new meanings, dimensions, and proactive uses due to innovations and changes in police deployment and the move towards more preventative policing strategies by law enforcement (Lum and Fachner 2008). The use of the patrol car for both proactive enforcement and investigation has become part of the tactical mission of many law enforcement agencies and has generated important crime prevention outcomes (see, e.g., Josi et al. 2000; McGarrell et al. 2001; Sherman et al. 1995; Weiss and McGarrell 1996). For example, traffic stops have been used for purposes of reducing gun carrying or detecting drug activity in high crime areas. Recently, a new use for traffic enforcement known as DDACTS, or Data-Driven Approaches to Crime and Traffic Safety,[14] links the locations of crime and traffic data to determine deployment strategies for police resources at specific places. Technologies such as license plate readers can automate a process of running vehicle tags that make it much easier and faster for officers to identify which vehicles to stop and whether the owner of a vehicle is wanted.

But with the use of traffic enforcement to achieve these broader proactive policing goals has come concerns about racial profiling and other discriminatory practices. Also relevant to our current discussion is that proactively patrolling crime "hot spots" and stopping vehicles may also increase the probability that officers will be involved in vehicular (or foot) pursuits considering the number of motivated offenders may be higher at these locations where crime concentrates. Thus, while many agencies have adopted restrictive pursuit policies, changes in deployment styles in policing may increase the occurrences when the decision to pursue must be made.

Given these complex issues regarding pursuits, has research in this area contributed to these discussions? Has there been a significant impact of research on pursuit practices and policy? This translational criminology brief examines the research data on police pursuits in the context of the current policing environment. We begin

---

[13] http://www.theiacp.org/tabid/299/Default.aspx?id=510&v=1.

[14] See http://www.nhtsa.gov/Driving+Safety/Enforcement+&+Justice+Services/Data-Driven+Approaches+to+Crime+and+Traffic+Safety+%28DDACTS%29.

with an overview of the issues faced by police and the public concerning pursuits and related legal issues. We review what we have learned from the research and its impact on policy and case law. We conclude by discussing the set of challenges faced by researchers and police managers in using research and analyses to inform law enforcement policy decisions.

A Historical Perspective on Police Pursuits: Police Traditions, Legal Cases, and Research

Law enforcement has always had to chase down fleeing criminals. Most of us first learned about police pursuits from television, the movies, and the media. In almost every western film, a law enforcement officer chases the "bad guy," usually on horseback, sometimes on foot. The bad guy keeps riding away until he is shot, his horse falls down, or he escapes. Once he is free from the sheriff or marshal, he slows down and goes about his routine business. While a few horses ridden by law enforcement officers probably ran over a few pedestrians or cut off other riders and stagecoaches, the chase was viewed as a way to fight crime.

Fast-forward to the days of motorized vehicles and police cars. *Bullitt*, *Gone in Sixty Seconds*, and *The Blues Brothers* filmed some of the more radical chases. *Miami Vice, Kojak, Law and Order*—it is hard to find a show about the police that does not have an exciting chase scene. However, many of us do not have a good handle on what really happens during a chase. Real pursuits do not always turn out as well as what we have become used to seeing on television and in the movies. There is no discussion about the consequences of a pursuit, much less a crash, beyond an arrest. There is no mention of injuries involving innocent bystanders or problems faced by the involved officers and their families.

Similarly, in the early days of policing, there was no real concern even within police departments about pursuits, and little concern about their consequences. Until the early 1980s, officers would chase suspects "until the wheels fell off." The chase was exciting and when it resulted in an apprehension, the tactic was a success. No risk was too great, and no offense was too minor. Little attention was given to the crashes, injuries, and deaths involving innocent bystanders who were in the wrong place at the wrong time.

However, a police training film produced and marketed in the 1970s by Motorola and narrated by *Dragnet's* "Sgt. Friday" (Jack Webb) began to change police attitudes. Using Los Angeles Police Department vehicles, the training video emphasized officer safety and suggested that the police have relatively little knowledge of the dynamics and dangers of driving. In an interesting demonstration of potential for harm, the video compares the relative power of a car crashing into a person and the force of a bullet hitting a person. It also makes clear how critical it is for police officers to receive driver training and guidance in decision making to keep them safe. The message of this video resonated throughout law enforcement: Emergency driving can be dangerous and officers need to know how to drive and make decisions about speeds and risks in order to avoid crashes and stay alive and maintain a level of public safety. Police departments began providing training on defensive and emergency driving skills, with a focus on technical proficiency (i.e., "Emergency Vehicle and Operations Course" or EVOC).

Our discussion of the legal issues related to pursuit is reserved for Chap. 2, but it is instructive to understand the legal thinking in the early 1950s in order to appreciate the history of pursuits and the influence of the law on police policy and management today. Interestingly, while civil suits questioned police actions in pursuits in the 1940s and 1950s, most of the decisions were concerned with the suspect and not the officer's driving or the causes of a crash. However, a thought-provoking and pivotal opinion was issued in Kentucky in 1952 in *Chambers v. Ideal Pure Milk Co.* (245 S.W.2d 589 (Ky. App. 1952)). Although the opinion centered on the suspect's decision to flee, it did open the door for more discussion on balancing risks versus benefits, proximate cause, and liability.

The *Chambers* case began at approximately 3:00 a.m. on February 10, 1941, when Milton Elmore, who was driving a horse-drawn, lighted milk wagon northward along Center Street in Owensboro, Kentucky, began to turn left in a westerly direction onto Fourth Street. A few moments earlier, police officers Robert Chambers and Jack Long had observed a parked car occupied by Wren Shearer, a person whose "bad reputation had become known to them." Shearer sped off to avoid an investigation by the police, and before Mr. Elmore completed his left turn, Shearer, who was fleeing at approximately 75 mph, crashed into the milk wagon, seriously injuring Mr. Elmore. Both Mr. Elmore and the Ideal Pure Milk Company sued officers Chambers and Long. At the end of the trial in October 1949, the jury awarded $588.83 to the Milk Company for its property damage, and $10,588.85 to Mr. Elmore as compensation for his injuries.

The officers challenged the verdict, and on appeal to the Kentucky Supreme Court, the Supreme Court reversed the trial court's decision. The Kentucky Supreme Court noted that: "Charged as they were with the obligation to enforce the law, the traffic laws included, they would have been derelict in their duty had they not pursued him. The police were performing their duty when Shearer, in gross violation of his duty to obey the speed laws, crashed into the milk wagon. To argue that the officers' pursuit caused Shearer to speed may be factually true, but it does not follow that the officers are liable at law for the results of Shearer's negligent speed. Police cannot be made insurers of the conduct of the culprits they chase. It is our conclusion that the action of the police was not the legal or proximate cause of the accident, and that the jury should have been instructed to find for the appellants" (590–591).

The *Chambers* decision was handed down by the court in 1952 and clearly indicated that while the actions of the officers most likely caused the offender to flee, the court should not legally hold the officers responsible for the actions of the fleeing suspect, even though he crashed into, and injured, an innocent bystander. During the more than 60 years since *Chambers*, the laws relating to police emergency and pursuit driving have changed dramatically, following to a certain degree early investigations into pursuits and how those studies framed later research.

In particular, during the late 1960s, a "watchdog" group called The Physicians for Automotive Safety, composed of emergency room physicians, released a report asserting that 70 % of all pursuits resulted in a crash, 50 % of all pursuits ended in serious injuries, and 20 % of pursuits resulted in a death (Physicians for Automotive Safety 1968; see also Fennessy et al. 1970). Unfortunately, the report relied more on anecdotal information, media reports, and undisclosed opinions rather than reliable research findings. Nonetheless, the group's comments caught the eye of some politicians and police administrators who became concerned that the report might impede their use of pursuits as a tactic. Criticism of the report's findings and faulty methods followed. As flawed as the report may have been, it was the only one published on the topic and its alarming findings did earn an audience.

To question the report, a second generation of "research" on pursuits was initiated in the 1980s that relied on quantitative data from police agencies. The California Highway Patrol (CHP) led the effort, collecting a variety of information from law enforcement agencies in California. Contrary to the findings published by the Physicians for Automotive Safety, the CHP reported that a "mere" 29 % of pursuits resulted in a crash, 11 % ended in injury, and 1 % resulted in a death (California Highway Patrol 1983). While the CHP study was also fraught with methodological shortcomings, it was the first of a series of studies that ultimately learned from the shortcomings of the earlier research and improved over time. Interestingly, while the Physicians for Automotive Safety concluded that pursuits were extremely dangerous and reform was necessary to save lives, the CHP concluded: "[A] very effective technique in apprehending pursued violators may be simply to follow the violator until he voluntarily stops or crashes" (1983, p. 17). In other words, it appeared that the CHP study concluded that a continued chase that would likely result in a crash could be the best way to respond to a fleeing suspect.

The conclusions from these two studies taken together with *Chambers* illustrate the confusion that surrounded pursuits during these early years of interest in analyzing them. While there was agreement that pursuits are dangerous, there were contradictory opinions about the source and cause of the danger, as well as competing ideas about what to do about the "newly found" problem. However, one constant dilemma remained to be addressed by both legal analysis and research: how to achieve balance between the need to apprehend the suspect (or the benefits of pursuit) and the risks or costs of pursuit.

Understanding the Costs and Benefits of Pursuits

While there remains no universally accepted answer to the question of how to balance the benefits and risks of pursuit, changes and improvements have occurred in our thinking about the balancing test since the CHP study. A number of cases, as presented in Chap. 2, not only provided legal precedent but also important guidance on the policies, training, supervision, and accountability of pursuits for law enforcement agencies. Some of that legal thinking has been influenced by a growing body of research and analysis on pursuits, detailed in Chap. 3. While this literature continues to show the limitations of police pursuits research given the lack of comprehensive and consistent data collection, it has also helped us better understand the nature, characteristics, and outcomes of pursuits. This information is important for understanding police pursuits in their proper context—as tactical operations with costs and benefits.

As an operational tactic, pursuit driving has not received a great deal of attention, and, as noted above, has only been of interest to researchers and managers since the 1970s. It is remarkable that such a potentially harmful tactic has not been scrutinized more thoroughly, as those who have studied it report there is no such thing as a trivial pursuit, and pursuit driving should be considered the most deadly weapon in a police officer's arsenal (Alpert and Anderson 1986). As the Motorola training film noted, when an officer engages in a chase in a high-powered, heavy motor vehicle, those vehicles become potentially dangerous and deadly weapons. The 1990s training guide for the California Peace Officer and Standards and Training (Cal POST) updated the notion of the force associated with pursuits (Learning Goal 6.3.1.0 [IADLEST 4.1 and 4.2]):

> The issue of deadly force most commonly arises in relation to the use of a law enforcement handgun. But which presents the greatest potential for causing bodily harm, 147 grains of a 9 mm bullet moving at 955 feet per second or a 4,000-pound vehicle travelling 60 miles per hour (88 feet per second)?
>
> The answer is your vehicle. A bullet traveling 955 feet per second develops 297 foot pounds of kinetic energy (kill power); the car traveling at 60 miles per hour develops 480,979 pounds of kinetic energy (kill power).

In other words, the manual emphasized that it does not really make a difference what the instrument of force is if the outcome is the same (i.e., someone can be killed or seriously injured).

The potential costs of a pursuit not only include the reckless driving of a suspect but also the fast, dangerous, and risky driving of one or more police officers. A significant challenge has also been the inability of law enforcement to stop the fleeing suspect without the use of a deadly force tactic such as ramming or shooting at the vehicle. The strategy that remains is the hope that a fleeing suspect will voluntarily stop and give up. While some fleeing suspects do stop after a short chase, most will continue to flee as long as the police officer continues to chase. The suspect's goal is to remain free and avoid arrest and, unless he has a death wish, he will often run until he believes he is safe, or crashes (Alpert 1997).

Indeed, the suspect, who has refused to heed the commands of the officer, has the primary responsibility to stop and pull over. The suspect is directing the pursuit by selecting the course, speed, and recklessness of the driving. However, any increased or continued recklessness on the part of the suspect may be affected by the officer's attempt to apprehend him, as noted in *Chambers*. Thus, the officer must temper his or her concerns for public safety with a natural desire to apprehend the suspect. Accordingly, the officer must become aware of personal capabilities and take into account environmental conditions that may affect his or her ability to protect lives. The police officer must factor into the decision-making process the risk created by the suspect's driving, the potential actions of innocent bystanders, passengers, and others who may become involved, and how his or her actions influence the suspect's driving. In addition, the officer must factor in the likelihood of apprehension in deciding whether to continue a chase, and how that apprehension will serve public safety.

Pursuing a suspect raises risks to all involved parties and innocent bystanders who happen to be in the wrong place at the wrong time. One way to help officers understand how to balance the risks and benefits of pursuit is to have them apply the same standards used in weighing the firing of a weapon in a situation where they may endanger innocent bystanders by shooting. Whenever an officer fires a weapon, he or she must be concerned that the bullet may accidentally hit an unintended target. By comparison, in pursuit, the officer has not only his or her vehicle to worry about, but also must consider the path taken by the pursued vehicle and the driver's capacity and skill to control it. Indeed, this risk is amplified by dangerous situations created by innocent drivers attempting to get out of harm's way (see Alpert and Fridell 1992).

While the costs of pursuits are high, there are also benefits to pursuits. Obviously, there is an ongoing need to apprehend law violators, also noted in *Chambers*. Many agencies use traffic control as an investigative tool, gaining a great deal of intelligence from these interactions with the public. Officers can check drivers and sometimes passengers for outstanding wants and warrants. The police do make arrests for more serious offenses as the result of traffic stops (and pursuits). One well-known example is the capture of Timothy McVeigh, within ninety minutes of his bombing of the Alfred P. Murrah Federal Building in Oklahoma City on April 19, 1995. Perhaps the most serious domestic terrorist in recent American history, McVeigh was stopped voluntarily when Oklahoma State Trooper Charlie Hanger turned on his emergency equipment when he observed a car driving on the freeway without a license plate.

If the police terminate their active attempt to apprehend a suspect, it is likely that the suspect will escape at least for the time being, and that some of these benefits might not be reaped. Some observers, including the authors of the 1983 California Highway Patrol Report, note that if the police do not chase suspects, there will be havoc on the roadways and police authority will erode. The proponents of pursuit also argue that suspects who flee have something more to hide than what the police are chasing them for. Because of this risk, they argue, police must continue to engage in pursuits, even though pursuits may put bystanders at risk of injury. But allowing suspects to escape comes with a price that may differ across types of offenders and communities. If minor traffic offenders or property offenders are allowed to escape, the social cost is not as high as if those who escape are violent or serious criminals.

These doubts add to the difficulty for an officer in understanding the potential cost–benefit of a pursuit. When a suspect refuses to stop, a routine encounter can turn quickly into a high-risk and dangerous pursuit where the officer's "show of authority" may affect the suspect's driving. As proactive enforcement may influence (i.e., increase) the number of suspects fleeing, there is a need for enhanced training for officers so they understand how their behavior affects the behavior of the fleeing suspect. If the suspect continues to act in a reckless fashion, becomes more reckless than before, or refuses to stop, it is the officer, relying on policy and training, who must determine the value of continuing the pursuit and its risks.

The question to pursue thus becomes an empirical one: Who do the police allow to flee and who do the police chase and apprehend? The question is confounded by the fact that often the officer does not know what the individual they are chasing has done. Rational thinking is further muddled by the excitement of the chase for both officers and suspects. The critical question is what benefit is derived from a chase compared to the risk of a crash, injury, or death, whether to members of the public, officers, or suspects. If the police are chasing a suspect who just raped a woman or shot someone, the reasonable, tolerable, and justifiable risks to the public obviously will be greater than the risk of chasing a suspect who stole a car, ran a red light, or simply had a bad reputation.

To assess these costs and benefits of pursuits, we need accountability—and accounting—about the use of this tactic. However, after a great deal of controversy and calls for strict pursuit policy we still have no national data on pursuits (or on police use of deadly force, for that matter). In 2012, 12 states had legislation requiring a repository of data on all pursuits. While there is uneven reporting among them, these states at least attempt to collect and analyze data on police pursuits. One of the oldest and most comprehensive programs of this type is the Minnesota Board of Peace Officer Standards and Training (POST), that in 1988 promulgated pursuit policy guidelines for statewide adoption that required all law enforcement agencies to collect and submit for analysis a minimum of 11 data elements concerning pursuits and their outcomes. This data set and others provide important information on the nature, frequency, and outcome of police pursuits. Nationally, the National Highway Traffic Safety Administration (NHTSA) as part of the Fatality Analysis Reporting System (FARS) collects data on police pursuit-related fatalities. The FARS data show that at least one person will die every day of the year in a police pursuit, with approximately 30 % of those deaths being an innocent bystander. These data also show that less than 2 % of the deaths are police officers and the majority of fatalities are those in vehicles fleeing the police (Hutson et al. 2007). While these data are likely incomplete and underreport pursuits, they still provide important information on the deaths that are reported and emphasize the importance of more comprehensive information for understanding the costs and benefits of pursuits.

Where Are We Now: Pursuits in a Period of Proactivity and Innovation

Cost and benefit calculations do not occur in a vacuum and have to be considered alongside the changing policing context. In particular, the police profession has developed from a "professional era," which emphasized standard operating procedures and quick response to 911 calls, to an era that is marked by more pressure for the police to be proactive and use more innovative patrol and investigative strategies. Before we detail in Chaps. 2 and 3 the legal precedent and research surrounding pursuits, it is worth examining how this change of context has also affected our understanding of pursuits.

Beginning in the late 1960s after a turbulent time for police, a loss of legitimacy with citizens, and the development and use of technology in policing, police began emphasizing a more professional and community-oriented approach to their craft. The professional era was characterized by policies, practices, and technologies that emphasized quick, efficient, fair, recorded, and standardized responses to calls for service (see Carlan 2006; Kelling and Moore 1988; Moore 1992; Reiss 1992). The main police function evolved into one in which a patrol officer's primary duty was to respond to 911 calls for service promptly and professionally as assigned from the radio- or computer-aided dispatch (CAD) systems. Officers were evaluated on their ability to respond to calls efficiently, fairly, and in a standardized manner. The advent of the patrol car and the move to mobile radios (as opposed to call boxes) became a regular fixture in police patrol deployment, which led to expectations of even faster response, putting more emphasis on this performance measure. These practices became the standard for policing in the professional era and created a deployment style and culture that was profoundly reactive to crime.

Although evaluation of reactive patrol and investigative tactics shows them to be largely ineffective in preventing or reducing crime (Lum et al. 2011b; Sherman et al. 1997; Sherman and Eck 2002; Weisburd and Eck 2004), this professional style permeated almost all aspects of many American law enforcement agencies and continues to be the dominant policing style today. Reactivity exists in patrol officers' responses to 911 calls, the case-by-case approach by which detectives handle investigations, as well as in other administrative matters such as officer discipline, performance measures, and supervision (Moore 1992). With regard to performance measures, officers today are still judged on how quickly they respond to calls for service, how many investigative cases they clear, and whether an arrest is made quickly. The emphasis on reactivity is also reflected in officer performance with regard to operating their vehicles. Before pursuits began to arise as a serious policy issue, they were considered a normal and acceptable way to respond to fleeing suspects, which was a natural consequence of professional and reactive policing. Miles driven per shift, maintenance and upkeep of a vehicle, and the number of collisions in which an officer is involved are used to gauge performance and ensure accountability.

However, a new era of policing began in the late 1980s and 1990s. Police have moved away from solely relying on this reactive approach and are now encouraged to use a more proactive policing style. In this new era, deployment paradigms such as community policing, problem-oriented policing, intelligence-led policing, predictive policing, legitimacy policing, hot spots policing, and evidence-based policing have emerged. All of these approaches emphasize that police should consider proactive and innovative ways to deal with crime, and criminals, including fleeing suspects. They are often anchored by the use of community input, information and data, analysis, and research to drive decision making, as well as the use of more proactive, focused, and tailored strategies. Performance measures are also different in this new era and include crime reduction and prevention, not just detection and apprehension.

For a variety of reasons, many police agencies are changing to more proactive policing in their function, organization, mandate to prevent crime, legitimacy, and accountability structures. While not embraced fully, these approaches require officers and their managers to think more about the crime control, prevention, and community consequences of their actions rather than merely responding to crimes and calls for service (see Lum 2009; Weisburd and Braga 2006). Officers are encouraged to use the time in between calls for service in proactive ways in order to reduce the volume of calls received in the first place. Strategies such as hot spots policing (see, e.g., Sherman and Weisburd 1995), problem solving (see, e.g., Braga et al. 1999; Taylor et al. 2011), or focused deterrence efforts at places (see, e.g., Sherman 1990; Sherman et al. 1995) are all examples of proactive approaches. Additionally, there is much greater use of mobile technologies (i.e., mobile computing, license plate recognition technologies, scanners, video cameras) to help facilitate these proactive interventions.

This move towards a proactive orientation reflects a change in context for pursuits. Officers who engage in these approaches now place themselves proactively in areas or situations where the probability either of having to chase individuals on foot or in their vehicles may be higher than during random, reactive patrols. Further, the choice of whether to stop an individual may now be more intelligence driven in addition to the basic reasonable suspicion required. Officers may have much more information about an individual before stopping them which might lead them to choose more higher-risk individuals to stop and ignore vehicles associated with registered owners who do not have criminal records. Thus, depending upon the source and type of information on which the police are operating, they may place themselves at higher risk of being in an encounter with an individual who has a propensity to flee. Within this new era of policing, officers may actually increase their risk of being involved in pursuits.

As part of crime prevention strategies in this new era, officers also use "pretext stops" and traffic enforcement as crime prevention strategies (Jang et al. 2012; Josi et al. 2000; Koper and Mayo-Wilson 2006; McGarrell et al. 2001, 2002; Sherman et al. 1995; Weiss and McGarrell 1996). In a pretext stop, officers stop individuals for minor traffic violations, but suspect a more serious crime. Under *Whren v. United States*,[15] the court deemed this practice constitutional, although many have argued this practice can lead to discriminatory behavior (see pp. 810–819 of *Whren* (1996)). The use of pretext stops, like the proactive tactics mentioned above, could place officers in situations of heightened risk for pursuits. These approaches can also affect officer cognition about the stop itself. For example, if an officer is conducting traffic stops in an area where prostitution is rampant, he or she may come to a very different conclusion about why a person would flee compared to an officer conducting stops in an area where gun crimes are common. Even if suspects in both scenarios flee for the same reason (e.g., the car was stolen), officers' perceptions based on their assigned tasks or understanding of a particular area may lead to very different thoughts, considerations, or mindsets.

Pretext stops are a relatively new practice, and sufficient research has not yet been conducted to understand all of their implications. However, we might gain insight from related research findings (Alpert and Dunham 1988) that found

---

[15] 517 U.S. 806 (1996).

pursuit-related crashes were more likely to occur when police were engaged in what they called "BOLO," or "be-on-the-lookout" activities, as opposed to traffic stops. Alpert and Dunham found that when police were instructed to watch for certain individuals, the targets were more likely to flee aggressively than citizens who would not stop for the police in a traffic stop. In other words, proactive targeting can increase the possibility of vehicular pursuits, because police are directing efforts at specific people and places.

In summary, in an era of greater proactivity and innovation, and given the serious consequences of police pursuits, police managers need to anticipate how these changing contexts of policing impact the costs and benefits of pursuits so that they can create better policies and training that address and control pursuits over time. In the chapters that follow, we examine both legal issues and research findings pertaining to the costs and benefits of pursuits. While each has influenced the development of pursuit policies, we still need a much stronger evidence base in this important area of policing.

Chapter 2
Pursuit Driving, the Law, and Liability

Lawsuits against the police for improper pursuit actions are a way for injured parties to seek relief, accountability, and a change in the ways police respond to fleeing suspects. While suing the police may censure or punish the officer and/or agency for wrongdoing, civil remedies are rarely a sufficient form of accountability as they do not always address flawed management, policies, or patterns of abuse, nor do they hold an individual officer financially responsible.[1] Nonetheless, a few important cases have shaped pursuit policy in the United States, some that have also been influenced by empirical research on pursuits. These cases emphasize the importance of generating more empirical knowledge and research about pursuits to better calculate their characteristics, costs, and benefits.

Historically, lawsuits involving pursuits have been brought in both federal and state courts. The cases in federal court have most often been filed under Title 42 U.S. Code §1983 that was enacted as part of the Civil Rights Act of 1871. Interestingly, the title is also known as the "Ku Klux Klan Act" because one of its primary purposes was to provide a civil remedy against the abuses that Klan members were committing in the southern states. The Act was intended to provide a private remedy for such violations of federal law and has subsequently been interpreted to create a class of tort liability. The Act creates no substantive rights but is a vehicle for suing a defendant protected by state law and is limited to those actors who exert authority derived from the government and who act as a representative of that government. The Act mandates that:

> Any person who, under color of any statute, ordinance, regulation, custom, or usage, of any State or Territory or the District of Columbia, subjects or causes to be subjected, any citizen of the United States or other person within the jurisdiction thereof to the deprivation of any

---

This chapter was partially adapted from: Alpert, G. and Smith, W. 2008. Police pursuits after *Scott v. Harris*: Far from ideal? *Ideas in American Policing Paper Series*. Washington, DC: Police Foundation.

[1] Often cities pay settlements to plaintiffs but do not admit liability for the misconduct and do not accept legal responsibility for the harm. In addition, settlements leave unresolved possible changes in policy and can impact officer morale.

G.P. Alpert and C. Lum, *Police Pursuit Driving: Policy and Research*, SpringerBriefs in Criminology, DOI 10.1007/978-1-4939-0712-0_2, © The Author(s) 2014

rights, privileges, or immunities secured by the Constitution and laws, shall be liable to the party injured in an action at law, suit in equity, or other proper proceeding for redress … .

After an initial flurry of activity involving slavery-related issues, the Act lay dormant until 1961 when the Supreme Court decided *Monroe v. Pape* (365 U.S. 167 (1961)). In *Monroe*, the Supreme Court held that a Chicago police officer was acting "under color of state law" even though his actions, which involved a search and seizure, violated state law. This was the first case in which the Supreme Court held a governmental agency liable when an official acted outside the scope of his authority as granted by state law. Plaintiffs had to overcome good faith immunity[2] until the Court decided *Monell v. Department of Social Services of New York* (436 U.S. 658 (1978)). After the decision in *Monroe v. Pape* and *Monell*, an extensive body of law developed to govern these claims, especially involving the Fourteenth and Fourth Amendments.

A major surge in litigation followed these decisions as many attorneys figured the Court had opened the floodgates to "deep pockets" and provided as well for the payment of all court costs[3] in these cases. For example, often an injury to a suspect or an innocent third party as the result of a pursuit was followed by a lawsuit alleging a violation of a federally secured right that the plaintiff sought to rectify under a Title 42 Section 1983 claim. The more serious the injury and damages, the more likely a suit would be filed. Countless civil rights suits were filed, with varying degrees of plaintiff creativity. However, there were few fact patterns that would predict a successful outcome for a plaintiff. Courts responded by applying different standards, interpreting agreed-upon standards differently, or handing down widely varied or inconsistent rulings on similar factual patterns.

By the early 2000s, the courts were contradicting each other, and practicing lawyers as well as legal scholars were mystified by the opinions. One of the few predictable rulings for a plaintiff in a civil rights suit involving pursuits relates to when a police officer used actions that reflected "means intentionally applied" (*Brower v. Inyo County* 489 U.S. 593 (1989)) to stop a fleeing suspect, such as ramming, a PIT maneuver,[4] or

---

[2] Good faith immunity generally protects government employees who perform discretionary acts from liability for civil damages, as long as their conduct does not violate an established statutory or constitutional right which is reasonably well known. A discretionary act is one in which there is no hard and fast rule as to what course of conduct should be taken. Discretion would be eliminated if there were a rule as to the course of conduct to follow. In addition to the qualified immunity from federal claims, states have statutes that grant a different type of qualified immunity to certain government employees from state law claims. These statutes protect employees who perform acts involving the use of discretion and judgment from personal liability in some states, except for those acts involving the operation, use, or maintenance of a motor vehicle, or the use of excessive force.

[3] 42 U.S.C. §1983.

[4] A Pursuit Immobilization Technique (PIT) is a maneuver that begins when a pursuing vehicle pulls alongside a fleeing vehicle so that either front quarter panel of the pursuing vehicle is aligned with the target vehicle's rear quarter panel. The pursuing officer is required to make momentary contact with the target vehicle's rear quarter panel, accelerating slightly and steering into it very briefly. The effect of the properly performed maneuver is that the rear wheels of the target vehicle lose traction, causing it to skid to a stop so that the pursuing officer or a backup vehicle is able to then block the target's escape and apprehend the suspect. Unfortunately, the process does not always work as planned. The PIT is designed to work safely at speeds slower than 40 MPH and in safe locations.

a stationary roadblock. In these situations, the federal courts would evaluate the officer's action as a "seizure" for purposes of a Fourth Amendment claim. The courts typically relied on the precedents established in *Tennessee v. Garner* (471 U.S. 1 (1985)) and *Graham v. Connor* (490 U.S.386, 388 (1989)) to analyze the damages of a pursuit.

County of Sacramento v. Lewis, 523 U.S. 833 (1998)

However, in the late 1990s, the US Supreme Court provided a somewhat puzzling analysis of the liability parameters of police pursuits under federal civil rights law using the opinions in *Brower v. County of Inyo* (489 U.S. 593 (1989)) and created a new standard in *County of Sacramento v. Lewis* (523 U.S. 833 (1998)) for Fourteenth Amendment claims. The *County of Sacramento v. Lewis* case began on May 22, 1990, at about 8:30 p.m., when Sacramento County Deputies James Everett Smith and Murray Stapp responded to a call to break up a fight. As the officers were completing their call and were about to leave, Deputy Stapp saw a motorcycle approaching at a high rate of speed. The motorcycle was operated by 18-year-old Brian Willard, who had a passenger—16-year-old Philip Lewis. Deputy Stapp turned on his overhead lights, yelled to the boys to stop, and pulled his patrol car closer to Deputy Smith's, attempting to block in the motorcycle. Instead of pulling over, Willard ignored the officer's commands and maneuvered his way between the two cars, taking off at a high rate of speed. Deputy Smith then put on his emergency overhead lights and sirens, and began a high-speed pursuit of the motorcycle. The chase lasted approximately 75 s and covered 1.3 miles of a residential neighborhood, reaching speeds of 100 mph in 30 mph zones. The motorcycle drove in and out of oncoming traffic, causing a few vehicles to swerve off the road. The chase ended when the motorcycle reached the top of a crest, tried to make a hard left turn, tipped over, skidded, and stopped. When Deputy Smith drove over the hill, he saw the motorcycle and slammed on his brakes. However, he was driving too close and too fast and was unable to stop in time, running over Lewis and killing him.

Lewis' parents filed suit against Sacramento County, the Sacramento County Sheriff's Department, and Deputy Smith under 42 U.S.C. §1983, alleging a deprivation of their son's Fourteenth Amendment substantive due process right to life. The specific question before the Court was: Does a police officer violate substantive due process by causing death through deliberate or reckless indifference to life in a high-speed chase aimed at apprehending a suspected offender? The unanimous Court decision changed the standard to one that required a plaintiff to show that the behavior of a police officer "shocked the conscience" and held: "High-speed chases with no intent to harm suspects physically or to worsen their legal plight do not give rise to liability under the Fourteenth Amendment" (854). The opinion continued:

> Smith was faced with a course of lawless behavior for which the police were not to blame. They had done nothing to cause Willard's high-speed driving in the first place, nothing to excuse his flouting of the commonly understood law enforcement authority to control traffic, and nothing (beyond a refusal to call off the chase) to encourage him to race through traffic at breakneck speed forcing other drivers out of their travel lanes. Willard's outrageous behavior was practically instantaneous, and so was Smith's instinctive response.

While prudence would have repressed the reaction, the officer's instinct was to do his job as a law enforcement officer, not to induce Willard's lawlessness, or to terrorize, cause harm, or kill. Prudence, that is, was subject to countervailing enforcement considerations, and while Smith exaggerated their demands, there is no reason to believe that they were tainted by an improper or malicious motive on his part. Regardless whether Smith's behavior offended the reasonableness held up by tort law or the balance struck in law enforcement's own codes of sound practice, it does not shock the conscience .... (at 834–835)

The *Lewis* decision essentially closed the door on successful allegations of constitutional deprivations of actions resulting from a police pursuit under the Fourteenth Amendment. Suits filed since are rare and settle outside of court. In order to gain any advantage for a defendant, the facts must be so outrageous that a jury might believe that an officer wanted to cause harm to the person they were chasing unrelated to the legitimate object of arrest or worsen their legal plight. Since *Lewis*, almost no realistic claims alleging a Fourteenth Amendment violation concerning a pursuit has been successful, leaving only a Fourth Amendment claim as a realistic remedy for a plaintiff looking to allege an unreasonable seizure.

Fourth Amendment

The use of the Fourth Amendment's protection against illegal seizures was the last federal remedy available for those who questioned the actions of police involved in pursuits. Relying on *Tennessee v. Garner* and *Graham v. Connor*, the courts determined the reasonableness of the officer's actions. The Fourth Amendment protects:

The right of the people to be secure in their persons, houses, papers, and effects, against unreasonable searches and seizures, shall not be violated, and no Warrants shall issue, but upon probable cause, supported by Oath or affirmation, and particularly describing the place to be searched, and the persons or things to be seized.

Interestingly, the federal courts left a better protection for the fleeing suspect who was "seized" illegally than the innocent bystander who was in the wrong place at the wrong time, even to be run over by a police car chasing a fleeing suspect.

The *Graham* decision, which built on *Garner*, required an objective inquiry into the officer's behavior that must consider the officer's perspective at the time, including the often "tense, uncertain, and rapidly evolving" circumstances of the event (*Graham v. Connor*, 490 U.S. 386, 396–397 (1989)). The Court determined that reasonable behavior was to be determined by balancing the intrusion on the individual's interests with the government's competing interests, by considering:

1. "the severity of the crime at issue,
2. whether the suspect poses an immediate threat to the safety of the officers or others,
3. whether he is actively resisting arrest ... or
4. [whether he is] attempting to evade arrest by flight." (at 396)

The Court's language in *Brower* (that "a seizure occurs when governmental termination of a person's movement is effected through means intentionally applied"), taken in conjunction with the holding in *Garner* that deadly force may not be used to seize a fleeing suspect unless the suspect poses a significant threat of death or serious physical injury to the officer or others, led many observers to conclude that the police use of such maneuvers as PIT and ramming against traffic or other nonviolent offenders would represent an unreasonable seizure, supporting Section 1983 liability. This belief was based on the balance between the level of offense committed by the suspect and the amount of government intrusion or force, which was a hallmark of the *Garner* decision. The case of *Scott v. Harris* (550 U.S. 372 (2007)) abruptly changed this belief.

Scott v. Harris, 550 U.S. 372 (2007)

On March 29, 2001, at approximately 10:40 p.m., Deputy Clinton Reynolds of the Coweta County Sheriff's Department (CCSD) in Georgia was stationed on Highway 34 when he clocked a vehicle driven by Victor Harris traveling 73 mph in a 55 mph zone. Reynolds decided to pursue Harris for speeding. As Harris sped away from the officer, he passed other motorists by crossing over double-yellow traffic control lines and also raced through a red traffic light. Reynolds radioed dispatch and reported that he was chasing a fleeing suspect, providing the license plate number of Harris' vehicle. Deputy Reynolds received the name and address of the owner of the car but did not broadcast any information about the underlying offense—speeding—for which he was chasing Harris. Based on the speeding offense and the fact that the car was known to be lawfully registered to Harris, Reynolds' initiation of the pursuit violated the sheriff department's vehicular pursuit policy. That policy did not authorize officers to engage in pursuits for offenses such as speeding if they had information about a fleeing suspect that would allow apprehension of the suspect later.

At the time of Reynolds' call to dispatch, Deputy Timothy Scott, also from Coweta County Sheriff's Department, was parked by a church about a mile away. Along with Reynolds, his assignment that evening was to assist undercover officers who were making a controlled buy of illegal drugs. Assuming the pursuit was in connection with the undercover operation, Deputy Scott joined the pursuit to assist Reynolds. Scott estimated that in order to join the pursuit he reached speeds in excess of 100 mph on the narrow two-lane road. From the evidence available in the record, it also appeared that he forced numerous motorists from the roadway in his efforts to join the pursuit of Harris.

The pursuit began in Coweta County and ultimately ended in Peachtree City in Fayette County near Harris' home. At one point, when the chase entered Peachtree City, Harris slowed his vehicle and entered an empty drugstore parking lot. Deputy Scott attempted to stop Harris, who despite bumping into Scott's patrol car remained undeterred and sped off again onto another road, Highway 74, where he again drove at high speeds, crossing double-yellow lines and running a red light.

As the pursuit left the parking lot, Scott requested to be the primary pursuit unit, stating over the radio, "Let me have him … my car's already tore up." Deputy Scott took over as the lead vehicle and then requested permission from his supervisor, Sgt. Fenninger, to use a PIT maneuver on Harris. The Coweta County Sheriff's Department had never trained its officers in applying the PIT maneuver. Sgt. Fenninger responded to Scott's request by stating over the radio, "Go ahead and take him out. Take him out." At the time of his approval to Scott, Fenninger was aware that there were no other vehicles or pedestrians in the area and that Harris posed no immediate threat to the officers or to others.

During the pursuit, Scott became concerned that both his and Harris' vehicles were moving too quickly to execute a PIT maneuver safely and instead picked a moment when no motorists or pedestrians appeared to be in the immediate area. He then rammed Harris's vehicle while they were traveling at approximately 90 mph. The ramming resulted in Harris losing control of his vehicle, rolling it down an embankment, and crashing. Because of the crash, Harris was rendered quadriplegic. Immediately after Deputy Scott rammed Harris' vehicle, Deputy Reynolds notified dispatch that there was a bad crash.

Harris filed suit under 42 U.S.C. §1983, alleging the use of excessive force resulting in an unreasonable seizure under the Fourth Amendment. The District Court denied Scott's summary judgment motion, which was based on a claim of qualified immunity. The Eleventh Circuit affirmed on appeal, concluding that Scott's actions could constitute "deadly force" and that the use of such force violates Harris' constitutional right to be free from excessive force during a seizure. The United States Supreme Court granted a writ of certiorari on the second prong of the immunity question, whether the law gave fair warning to Scott that his conduct was unlawful, and heard oral arguments. It published its written decision on April 30, 2007, reversing the denial of qualified immunity by the Eleventh Circuit and granting summary judgment to Deputy Scott.

A unique feature of the Supreme Court opinion was the reliance on the videotape that was taken from Scott's patrol car. All but one of the justices agreed that Harris drove in a dangerous and reckless manner and presented a real threat to any driver on the roadway. The majority opinion, in an exceptional departure from the Court's standard of review of District Court factual determinations, viewed Harris' version of the events underlying the pursuit as being "so utterly discredited by the record (videotape) that no reasonable jury could have believed him" (at 1775, 1776). The high court's *de novo* factual review is even more interesting in that the Eleventh Circuit Court of Appeals reviewed the same videotape as the District Court and reached the same opinion as the lower court: that Harris' depiction of the events was credible and warranted consideration by a jury, not disposition by summary judgment. The Supreme Court stated that a review of the videotape might cause an observer versed in police practices and procedures to question the actions of the police officers who, even in the words of the majority, were "forced to engage in the same hazardous maneuvers just to keep up" (at 1775). Nonetheless, the Court decided that the videotape provided incontrovertible evidence that Harris presented a threat to others on the road and that the only question remaining for resolution was whether Scott's use of force to eliminate the threat was "objectively reasonable."

The underlying act of speeding played little, if any, role in the majority's assessment of the appropriateness of the level of force used by Scott. Instead, the court focused on the threat it believed Harris posed to the public. The Court rejected Harris' request that it analyze Scott's actions as an application of deadly force set out in *Tennessee v. Garner* and instead chastised both Harris and the Court of Appeals for seeking to apply *Garner* as an "on/off switch that triggers rigid preconditions whenever an officer's actions constitute 'deadly force'" (at 1777). The Court's opinion noted that *Garner* did not create a rule, but "was simply an application of the Fourth Amendment's 'reasonableness' test, to the use of a particular type of force in a particular situation" (1777, citations omitted). The majority opinion drew no distinction between excessive use of force and the use of deadly force in its analysis of Deputy Scott's behavior. The Court's opinion rested not upon whether the force used was deadly, only whether it was reasonable. The Court also gave little attention to the fact that Harris' underlying offense was speeding and instead voiced its greatest concern over the view that the act of fleeing and the nature of his driving were a threat to everyone, and that those who flee from the police recklessly implicitly authorize officers to seize them with the force necessary. In sharing the basis for its opinion, the Court offered the following contemplation:

> So how does a court go about weighing the perhaps lesser probability of injuring or killing numerous bystanders against the perhaps larger probability of injuring or killing a single person? We think it appropriate in this process to take into account not only the number of lives at risk, but also their relative culpability. It was respondent, after all, who intentionally placed himself and the public in danger by unlawfully engaging in the reckless, high-speed flight that ultimately produced the choice between two evils that Scott confronted. Multiple police cars, with blue lights flashing and sirens blaring, had been chasing respondent for nearly 10 miles, but he ignored their warning to stop. By contrast, those who might have been harmed had Scott not taken the action he did were entirely innocent. We have little difficulty in concluding it was reasonable for Scott to take the action that he did (at 1778).

The Court decided the case on grounds of qualified immunity, as the facts as represented by each side had never been presented to a jury. Interestingly, the unique element in the case was the Court's deference to the videotape it repeatedly mentions. The Court viewed the videotape of the chase during oral argument and posted a link to it on the Court's website for the public to view. The significance of the tape is its role in the Court's *de novo* determination of the facts considered in the summary judgment motion. In a summary judgment motion, as the Court notes, the trial court is "required to view the facts and draw reasonable inferences 'in the light most favorable to the party opposing the [summary judgment] motion.' In qualified immunity cases, this usually means adopting (as the Court of Appeals did here) the plaintiff's version of the facts." (at 1774, citations omitted). In this case, however, the Court noted "an added wrinkle… [the] existence in the record of a videotape capturing the events in question" (at 1775). Relying on a single videotape, the Court ruled that Harris' version of the facts was blatantly contradicted and went on to indicate that courts should not rely on the plaintiff's statement where such records, as videotapes, exist. Interestingly, there is no mention of three other police tapes that had been entered into the record and show different portions of the pursuit (Stevens, J. dissenting at 1785, footnote 7).

Scott v. Harris and the Cost–Benefit Calculation of Pursuits

At the end of the day, the Court balanced the risk of harm created by Scott's action of ramming Harris' vehicle with the threat created by Harris' fleeing from Scott. Even though the Court admitted that there is no obvious way to quantify these risks, it noted that Harris "posed an actual and imminent threat to the lives of any pedestrians who might have been present, to other civilian motorists, and to the officers involved in the chase" (at 1778). While the Court noted that Deputy Scott's actions posed a high likelihood of serious injury or death to Harris, although not specifically declaring Scott's action as an application of deadly force, it stated that the action did not pose the near certainty of death posed by shooting a fleeing felon in the back of the head or pulling next to a fleeing motorist's car and shooting the driver (at 1778). Essentially, the Court approached its analysis of the reasonableness of an application of force through a process of quantification of the level of force based on likely outcome—something it states there is no obvious way to do. The Court explained the logic by considering the number of lives at risk and the relative culpability of those involved. In that Harris disobeyed the initial order by Reynolds to stop, he intentionally placed himself and others at great risk. By contrast, members of the public who might find themselves at the wrong place at the wrong time were clearly innocent of any wrongdoing. Under this analysis, the wrongdoer, irrespective of the underlying offense, shoulders the total responsibility for the consequences of the actions of all involved parties, including the police. Appropriately, the Court shifts any blame away from the innocent bystanders, but it places total blame and culpability on the fleeing suspect.

What is missing from the equation is the responsibility of the police officers given what we know about the dynamics of pursuit. First, the opinion includes language that questions what Harris, or any other fleeing suspect, might have done or would do if the police end a pursuit. The Court was also silent on the established dynamics of pursuit and ignores research findings that have been published on the likelihood that a suspect will slow down and reduce the risk to the public, himself, and the police should the police terminate pursuit (see Alpert et al. 2000; California Highway Patrol 1983; see also Chap. 3 in this monograph).

Second, the Court did not see fit to address the great risk that Scott's ramming of Harris' car posed for the innocent motorists the Court claims the act was intended to protect. In its *de novo* factual determination of the "actual and imminent threat to the lives of any pedestrians who might have been present," the Court neglects, or refuses to consider, the role of Scott in this calculus. Substituting its view of a single videotape for evaluation of Scott's conduct by those more familiar with acceptable police *operational* practices, the Court sidesteps the issue of potential harm to the public or the reasonableness of the ramming of Harris' vehicle from a police practices perspective, and instead focuses on the relative culpability of Harris. The record in the case establishes that Harris' vehicle veered to the right and collided with a telephone pole after Deputy Scott rammed it. Because no innocent driver, passenger, or pedestrian was injured, the Court was able to sidestep the issue of actual harm.

Likewise ignored by the Court was the fact that ramming a vehicle at 90 mph disables the driver of the target vehicle's ability to steer or guide it. Based on the angle and height of the ramming vehicle, a rammed vehicle can be forced to travel in any number of directions. In this case, it could just as easily have veered to the left and across the median and into oncoming lanes of traffic. Thus, while the Court underpins its opinion on the protection of innocent third parties and the moral culpability of Harris, the fact remains, even under the Court's own analysis, that the missile put into motion by Scott's ramming could as easily have injured those parties as protect them. The irony of the Court's factual reevaluation in the case is that the analysis does precious little to provide protection to a potentially endangered public and a great deal to "green light" unrestrained police vehicular tactics in those agencies not holding a tight rein on their officers. The Court's own statements confirm that the practice of "pursue until the wheels fall off," a practice that so many law enforcement driving professionals and administrators have worked to change, could be more acceptable under federal law:

> A police officer's attempt to terminate a dangerous high-speed car chase that threatens the lives of innocent bystanders does not violate the Fourth Amendment, even when it places the fleeing motorist at risk of serious injury or death (at 1779).

In theory, the police can stop motorists who flee from them and threaten the lives of innocent bystanders with whatever force is necessary. If a suspect were to flee from the police on a highway while driving at high speed and the officer shot and killed the suspect under the guise of protecting the innocent motoring public, it is fairly clear that there would be no constitutional liability for the police under Harris. In fact, after Harris, any use of force or deadly force to stop a fleeing motorist when there is probable cause to believe he or she is posing a serious threat to the public is going to be justified under the Fourth Amendment. The key issue appears to be how the risk created by the continued flight of the suspect driver is determined by the officers involved (*Allen v. City of West Memphis*, No. 11-5266, U.S. Court of Appeals for the Sixth Circuit, October 9 2012).

Unfortunately, there is no bright line or formula to determine the risk created by the continued flight of a motorist. Unless there is probable cause that a fleeing suspect has committed a violent crime, it is difficult to determine that a reasonable officer would consider continued flight a clear risk to others. In fact, footnote 11 of the *Scott v. Harris* opinion states:

> Contrary to Justice Stevens' assertions, we do not "assum[e] that dangers caused by flight from a police pursuit will continue after the pursuit ends," post, at 6, nor do we make any "factual assumptions," post, at 5, with respect to what would have happened if the police had gone home. We simply point out the uncertainties regarding what would have happened, in response to respondent's factual assumption that the high-speed flight would have ended.

Since the decision in *Scott v. Harris*, a few cases in federal circuits have made it past the summary judgment stage, but none has gone to trial. Some of the settlements have been substantial, but there has been insignificant clarification of the law. Perhaps one of the most important cases comes from the Fifth Circuit. In *Lytle v. Bexar County* (560 F.3d 404, 414 (5th Cir. 2009), the court ruled, "it is unreasonable for a police officer to use deadly force against a fleeing felon who does not pose a sufficient threat of harm to the officer or others" (at 417). While this general principle is correct, it still begs the question of what constitutes a sufficient threat. In *Lytle*, the police shot at a fleeing vehicle that posed "some threat of harm" (at 415). That threat, however, consisted of driving at high speeds through a residential area. "… the Court's decision in *Scott* stated that an officer's attempt to end a high-speed chase that threatens lives of innocent bystanders, even if it places the fleeing motorist at serious risk of death, did not declare open season on suspects fleeing in motor vehicles" (Id. at 415). The court referenced Justice Ginsburg's concurring opinion in *Scott v. Harris* in which she pointed out that *Scott* did not "articulat[e] a mechanical, per se rule" but was situation specific and was concerned with the lives and well-being of those who were not fleeing but were acting in lawful ways and happened to be at the wrong place at the wrong time, or those who were in pursuit of the fleeing suspect (*Scott* at 1779).

One of the more recent cases that almost went to trial was *Walker v. Davis* (649 F 3d 502 (6th Cir. 2011)). In that case, an officer in rural Kentucky clocked Thomas Germany riding his motorcycle at 70 mph in a 55 mph zone. That officer (who was not a defendant in the case) tried to pull Germany over for speeding, but Germany refused to stop. Another officer, Danny Davis, heard about the pursuit over the radio. As Germany approached Davis' location, Davis blocked the road with his cruiser. After Germany maneuvered around him, Davis began his pursuit of Germany. The entire pursuit lasted about 5 min and took place on empty stretches of highway. Germany never went above 60 mph during the chase itself. He ran one red light.

Germany eventually turned off the road and cut across a muddy field. Davis followed close behind in his cruiser. According to the Estate's reconstruction expert—who analyzed, among other things, the location of paint transfers between the two vehicles— Davis then intentionally rammed Germany's motorcycle. Germany was thrown from the motorcycle and dragged underneath the cruiser, which crushed him to death.

The summary judgment for the Allen County, Kentucky, Sheriff's Office was denied because ramming Germany on a motorcycle was potentially deadly force and a possible violation of his Fourth Amendment rights. The court noted that it was a question for the jury whether the ramming was an intentional and therefore illegal act:

> It has been settled law for a generation that, under the Fourth Amendment, "[w]here a suspect poses no immediate threat to the officer and no threat to others, the harm resulting from failing to apprehend him does not justify the use of deadly force to do so." *Tennessee v. Garner*, 471 U.S. 1, 11, 105 S. Ct. 1694, 85 L. Ed. 2d 1 (1985). Here, Germany posed no immediate threat to anyone as he rode his motorcycle across an empty field in the middle of the night in rural Kentucky. That fact, among others, renders this case patently distinguishable from *Scott v. Harris*, 550 U.S. 372, 127 S. Ct. 1769, 167 L. Ed. 2d 686 (2007), in which Harris had led the police on a "Hollywood-style car chase of the most frightening sort, placing police officers and innocent bystanders alike at great risk of serious injury." *Id.* at 380. The chase here was a sleeper by comparison.
>
> Nor does it matter that, at the time of Davis's actions, there were few, if any, reported cases in which police cruisers intentionally rammed motorcycles. It is only common sense—and obviously so—that intentionally ramming a motorcycle with a police cruiser involves the application of potentially deadly force. This case is thus governed by the rule that "general statements of the law are capable of giving clear and fair warning to officers

even where the very action in question has not previously been held unlawful." *Smith v. Cupp*, 430 F.3d 766, 776–77 (6th Cir. 2005) (internal marks omitted)" (at 505).

The case was headed to trial, but was settled in the summer of 2012 at the last hour. This course has been the path for most post-*Scott v. Harris* Fourth Amendment claims and is likely to be followed in the future. If the claim passes the summary judgment stage, then the parties must decide whether to settle. However, more generally, the federal courts have closed their doors to Constitutional claims concerning pursuits and direct litigation to state court claims.[5]

State Court Claims

The *Scott v. Harris* court decision is only relevant to federal claims made by the fleeing suspect and does not impact state law claims made by those injured because of a pursuit. Actions brought against an officer or the employing agencies under state law are based on allegations of some level of negligence that was a proximate cause of damage. Simple negligence, perhaps the most common standard found among the states, is a level of behavior (or inaction) based upon a failure to comply with the duty of care of a reasonable officer. The specific definition or standards are established by the states and it is incumbent upon the plaintiff to show that the defendant has breached the particular standard of care owed to him or her. Standards higher than negligence exist and include reckless disregard of the consequences of conduct, willful and wanton misconduct, and deliberate indifference. While these standards are somewhat vague, courts have defined them or at least provided examples of behavior they believe satisfy the requirement.[6]

Regardless of whether the tort alleged involves an intentional or negligent act, a plaintiff may not recover for injury if there was no duty owed to the plaintiff by the officer who caused the injury. The term "duty," as used here, means that there was some obligation recognized by the law for the officer to behave in a particular

---

[5] In November 2013, The U.S. Supreme Court granted certiorari in Plumhoff v. Rickard, No. 12–1117 (2014), an unpublished decision in Estate of Allen v. City of West Memphis, 509 Fed. App'x 388 (6th Cir. 2012). The Court agreed to review the July 2004 case involving a chase into Memphis by West Memphis police officers in which the fleeing car's occupants were killed by police gunfire. The Supreme Court will likely reverse the Sixth Circuit and declare that its approach is fundamentally inconsistent with Scott.

[6] For example, a reasonable summary of negligence follows: (1) A legal duty or obligation, requiring the person to conform to a certain standard of conduct, for the protection of others against unreasonable risks; (2) A failure on the person's part to conform to the standard required: a breach of the duty; (3) A reasonably close causal connection between the conduct and the resulting injury, commonly known as "proximate cause"; (4) Actual damages or a loss resulting from the failure to perform a legal duty. From a practical standpoint, negligence in a pursuit may come about in any number of ways, to include the three following situations: (1) An officer violates an applicable state statute that creates a duty to act or not act; (2) An officer violates pertinent department policy which creates a duty to act or not act; and/or (3) An officer violates an established duty to use "due care" generally.

fashion towards the person who was ultimately injured. The law recognizes generally that if there was no duty to the injured on the part of a law enforcement officer, then there can be no liability for the officer or the employer.

Rather than attempt to provide a state-by-state comparison of pursuit standards and laws, we can examine one pursuit case filed in Tennessee, *Swindle v. City of Memphis* (Case No. CT-005342-09—Div. IX), which involves a number of issues of interest to researchers and practitioners.[7] This pursuit and the subsequent lawsuit are noteworthy because of multiple allegations of wrongdoing, the nature and type of evidence that was available, and the complexities that were involved in the chase. As noted above, many cases are settled before trial and the facts are never heard by a fact finder, whether a judge or jury. This case is representative of those that are "worked up" for trial and include volumes of discovery, including reports, depositions, expert reports, and video tapes.

Swindle involved a high-speed pursuit of a suspected car thief by members of the Memphis Police Department (MPD) on July 20, 2009, which resulted in the death of Iyana Swindle and her unborn child. On July 20, 2009, the MPD received a dispatch that a vehicle had been stolen from a rental car company. The dispatcher provided a description of the suspect, assigning Officer Mario Tate to investigate the complaint. At the rental car company, Tate spoke with company representatives and was shown a videotape that captured the vehicle being stolen by the suspect. Employees of the rental car company informed Tate that the stolen vehicle was equipped with a GPS unit. Importantly, the vehicle stolen was not taken by force or with the use of a weapon and, therefore, there was no report that a violent felony had been committed.

The rental car company had provided the MPD dispatcher with information pertaining to the location and direction of travel of the stolen vehicle, and the dispatcher broadcast that over the radio, along with a description of the vehicle and suspect. Shortly thereafter, Officer Tate spoke with Officer Tukes by car-to-car radio and cell phone about the location of the stolen vehicle. During this time Tukes had also been communicating with Detective Gaylor from the auto-theft division of the MPD, and Officer Bond about the car theft. Based on these discussions about the theft and description of the suspect, Tukes believed that he knew the person who had committed the car theft—Jarvis Evans. Confirming this point was the fact that the stolen vehicle was parked at a location where Jarvis Evans used to live. Significantly, the vehicle was stopped at this location for over 30 min based on the GPS tracking printout. Tukes was also provided with information over the radio that Evans was known to "run from police." Finally, Tukes was informed that Evans had active warrants out for previous car thefts. Despite the fact that the stolen vehicle was stopped for a substantial period of time, Tukes did not attempt to apprehend the suspect when the vehicle was stopped because he wanted to make sure that he could arrest

---

[7] The case, *Swindle v. City of Memphis, TN. Case No. CT-005342-09—Div. IX* was filed by Attorney Andrew C. Clarke, a well-known and well-respected attorney who has extensive experience in police pursuit matters. This section of the chapter comes directly from his court brief, with permission.

the suspect while driving the stolen vehicle and charge him with more serious crimes than if he were not driving the car.

After Tukes was informed that the car was moving, he continued to speak with Tate, who was providing information on the location of the vehicle based on the GPS tracking device. Tate informed Tukes that the vehicle was stopped at a convenience store at Fairway and South Third Street. Tukes requested additional police vehicles to proceed to that area without lights and sirens because Evans was known to flee. As Officer Tukes made it to the area of the convenience store, Officer Campbell and his passenger, Officer Green, were in their police vehicle approaching the corner of the convenience store. Tukes and Campbell observed the stolen vehicle in the parking lot of the convenience store. Campbell then saw the suspect leave the convenience store. Campbell motioned the suspect to his vehicle. Tukes testified that he recognized the suspect as Jarvis Evans.

Evans jumped into the stolen vehicle and drove off at a high rate of speed around the convenience store, ran through the intersection at Fairway and Third Street, and took off northbound on Third Street. Officer Campbell immediately gave chase. It is unclear whether Campbell turned on his police lights and sirens at this point or at any point during the pursuit. However, Memphis' sworn Interrogatory Responses indicate that Campbell activated his lights and sirens at this point. Tukes put on his lights and sirens, did a U-turn through heavy traffic and became the second vehicle in the pursuit. Campbell and Tukes continued pursuing Evans to the intersection of South Third and Mitchell, where Evans turned left. Campbell and Tukes also turned left at the intersection of South Third and Mitchell while still pursuing Evans. At the intersection of South Mitchell and Horn Lake Road, Evans went through the intersection and collided with a vehicle being driven by Iyana Swindle. As a result of that collision, Ms. Swindle, who was 15 weeks pregnant at the time, was killed.

The Memphis Police Department had a pursuit policy that clearly acknowledges that pursuits are inherently dangerous and significantly restricted their application to circumstances in which an officer has probable cause to believe that the suspect has committed a violent felony. Thus, MPD policy strictly prohibits pursuits of traffic offenders and suspects believed to have committed property crimes, including car theft. The City of Memphis in its internal affairs investigation found that Officers Tukes and Campbell violated the pursuit policy.

Based on the pre-pursuit facts, the plaintiff had to show that any pursuit of the fleeing suspect was unreasonable, as the suspect was not accused of committing any violent felony. The plaintiff also had to demonstrate that there were numerous other methods of apprehending the stolen vehicle and the suspect later without exposing the public to the dangers of a pursuit under nationally recognized law enforcement standards and MPD pursuit policy. In addition, she had to convince the fact finder that because the stolen vehicle was equipped with a GPS tracking device, there was absolutely no need to pursue the suspect, as the vehicle could have been retrieved later without exposing the public to the inherent dangers of the pursuit. Further, proof had to be demonstrated that there was no need to pursue because the officers had both a description of the suspect and a videotape of the crime. Officers Campbell, Green, and Tukes observed Evans getting into the stolen vehicle that would make later apprehension and prosecution of Evans probable without exposing the public to the dangers of the pursuit. The plaintiff had to demonstrate that the decision to initiate a pursuit of Evans under the circumstances of this case violated nationally recognized law enforcement standards and the MPD Pursuit Policy and was a proximate cause of the crash between Evans and Swindle, which resulted in the death of Ms. Swindle and her unborn child.

In 2011, the case went to trial in Memphis and the court awarded the estate of Ms. Swindle more than a million dollars. The court found the City of Memphis to be 35 % responsible for the damages, and the fleeing suspect to be 65 % responsible.

The Swindle case raises a variety of issues that can be addressed by research to help guide agencies and courts in the assessment of a pursuit. First, the case involves a stolen car fitted with a GPS tracking system. Logic informs us that the use of a GPS tracking system would remove the need to pursue a vehicle. While studies may not have been conducted on the impact of a GPS on the outcome of a pursuit, research has been conducted on the use of helicopters that involve an early method of tracking vehicles. Research results indicate an almost perfect record of apprehension without a crash when a helicopter is involved in a pursuit (Alpert 1998a). It would be a rather simple analysis to determine the comparative rate of apprehension and negative outcome between vehicles with GPS systems and those without. Conventional wisdom would follow the logic of the helicopter and suggest that when a vehicle has a GPS system, all the police have to do is follow it until it stops and apprehend the driver and passengers without a dangerous pursuit.

The police knew the suspected thief and had the ability to apprehend him when he was not in control of a vehicle. Conventional wisdom and research findings show the relative lack of danger when attempting to apprehend a suspect outside of a vehicle compared to those situations where the suspect has control of one (Alpert 1998b). While the officers indicated they wanted to observe him driving so he could be arrested on more serious charges, they could have used tactics to block-in the vehicle or disable it. Overall, the decision to become involved in an active pursuit of this suspect, under these conditions, was a violation of the officers' departmental policy and customary police practice and exposed the officers and their agency to civil liability.

The Role of Research in Legal Decisions

The federal and state cases illustrate many decisions law enforcement officers have to make regarding the costs and benefits of pursuits. The *Swindle* case is a good example of where research findings could provide information for managers and trainers that could be used to educate and train officers to help guide their decisions and avoid tragedy. The examples of *Scott v. Harris, Lytle v. Bexar County, and Walker v. Davis* all emphasize the need for high-quality information about the costs, benefits, and outcomes of pursuits to help both courts make decisions and law enforcement make better policy. Instead of best guessing, hunches, and "Monday-morning quarterbacking," there is research evidence and empirical knowledge that can answer the many hypothetical questions that are posed by analysis of these legal decisions.

However, most of the high-profile pursuit cases in federal courts have been decided not on empirical data but based on the beliefs and philosophies of the judges and justices. One recent case in which research was relied upon is *Sykes v. United States* (131 S. Ct. 2267 (2011)), in which Justice Thomas in his concurring opinion as well as Justices Kagan and Ginsberg in their dissenting opinion cited research findings from Lum and Fachner (2008) and Schultz et al. (2009). In *Sykes*, the dissenting justices point out that research knowledge does exist about the harm that could be caused by police pursuits, but also reiterated what researchers have been saying: that more comprehensive study is needed.[8] But generally, social science data, which can show the likelihood of pursuits resulting in crashes or injuries as well as costs of negative outcomes, are conspicuously absent from court decisions.

However, the decisions discussed in this chapter are important in building the evidence-base for police pursuits research. They serve to provide important information and questions to guide the policies, training, supervision, accountability, and research related to pursuits for law enforcement agencies. Combined with existing research on pursuit driving, the lessons learned from these legal decisions and analyses can help police managers and leaders develop their pursuit management plans. The next chapter moves from what we know about the law to what we have learned from research about pursuits and pursuit management.

---

[8] Interestingly, the court used the statistic of 4 % of *injury* from pursuits found by Lum and Fachner, but do not discuss how 24 % of pursuits result in a negative outcome (i.e., injury, crashes, accidents, property damage).

Chapter 3
The Evidence Base of Police Pursuits

While issues raised in pursuit litigation have played an important role shaping how courts balance the costs and benefits of pursuits, empirical research on pursuits can, and has, also contributed. Knowing how often and under what conditions pursuits result in property damage, injuries, and death can help us better calculate costs. Similarly, understanding how often and under what conditions pursuits are initiated, and when they result in an apprehension, provides us with a better understanding of the public safety benefits. Evaluation research can further determine whether changes in pursuit policies or the use of specific technologies and tactics (PIT maneuver, spike strips, helicopters, etc.) have any impact on outcomes (arrests, crashes, injuries).

Pursuit reporting, data collection, research, and analysis have come a long way since the Physicians for Automotive Safety report and the California Highway Patrol's study in 1983 discussed in Chap. 1. Although these early studies were methodologically limited, they emphasized the importance of empirical analysis of police pursuits and the need for more systematic collection of pursuit data.

The research efforts that followed documented pursuits and their characteristics as well as noted the need for more comprehensive and accurate reporting (Alpert et al. 2000; Lum and Fachner 2008). We will discuss in the next chapter whether this growing evidence on police pursuits has had a significant influence on policy or court opinions. Here, we present a brief review of the empirical studies on pursuit data, which provide a general understanding about the nature, characteristics, and outcomes of pursuit driving.

This chapter builds on the second author's report to the International Association of Chiefs of Police regarding research on police pursuits: Lum, C. and Fachner, G. 2008. Police pursuits in an age of innovation and reform. Alexandria, VA: International Association of Chiefs of Police. New research is included, and analysis and commentary is updated regarding the state of empirical research of police pursuits.

Empirical Studies of Police Pursuits

Adding to the data collected by Lum and Fachner in 2008 (which reported on 33 pursuit studies), we located 11 additional pursuit studies for a total of 44 studies that have examined empirical data about pursuits since the Physicians report. These studies are listed in Table 3.1 and include their citation, the location of the study, the years data on pursuits were collected, the number of pursuits studied, a brief summary of the study, and its findings. We believe this is the most comprehensive list of empirical studies of pursuits to date.[1]

One can see how pursuit studies have varied in location, scope, and focus since the Physicians for Automobile Safety study. Almost 80 % ($n = 35$) of the 44 studies examine pursuits in the United States, including data from Florida, California, Maryland, New York, Kentucky, Michigan, Illinois, South Carolina, Nebraska, Arizona, Texas, and Minnesota. Nine studies were conducted in the United Kingdom and Australia. In some cases, researchers examined multiple agencies and their data. Periods in which pursuits were analyzed include records dating back to the 1970s and include data as recent as 2010 (although most studies took place in the late 1980s and early 1990s). Studies have examined databases of pursuits as small as 17 (Alpert et al. 1997) and as large as 20,378 (Bayless and Osborne 1998). Three of the 44 studies that we include in Table 3.1 did not study all pursuits in a jurisdiction, but only pursuits that resulted in fatalities (Australian Institute of Criminology 2013; Hutson et al. 2007; Rivara and Mack 2004). In at least ten of the studies reported, authors looked at other units of analysis in addition to pursuits (such as pursuits that resulted in fatalities, or officers and suspects involved in pursuits).

The results of this research provide us with a number of important insights. The first is perhaps the most obvious: Empirical studies on pursuits are available to help inform law enforcement agencies as they develop policies and manage pursuits. From this body of research, agencies can get a sense of what conditions increase or decrease the likelihood of a negative outcome and the greatest chance of apprehension. The studies of pursuits resulting in fatalities are especially profound and provide agencies with significant information about the types of events that have fatal outcomes. This type of evidence and information is essential in supporting law enforcement decision making, especially for high-risk police activities that have such serious consequences (Alpert 1988).

These studies also provide descriptive statistics and sometimes correlational and predictive analyses of many aspects of police pursuits, illustrating the wide array of information that can be collected. Such factors include reasons why pursuits are initiated (offense or crime), characteristics of the pursuit situation (time of day, weather, road conditions, speeds of vehicles, length of the pursuit, number and type of vehicles, among others), and the outcomes of pursuits (arrests and charges, damages, injuries, and deaths). Information collected about the drivers (age, gender, driving record, employment status, officer time-in-service, arrest record of the

---

[1] The studies in Table 3.1 do not include qualitative or legal examinations of specific pursuits or studies of pursuit policies.

Table 3.1 Empirical studies of police pursuit data

Author(s) and year of study	Location of study	Years data were analyzed	Number pursuits studied	Other units studied	Brief summary	Key findings
Alpert (1987)	Metro-Dade (FL) PD	1985–1986	398		Analyzed characteristics and outcomes of police pursuits in the context of Metro-Dade Police Department's pursuit policy; compared to the California Highway Patrol (CHP)	33 % of pursuits resulted in an accident, with 14 % ending in personal injuries, and 62 % leading to an arrest. The comparison, CHP, saw 29 % of pursuits ending in accidents, 11 % resulting in injuries, and 77 % resulting in apprehension
Alpert and Dunham (1988, 1990)	Metro-Dade (FL) and Miami PDs	1985–1987	952		Analysis of accidents, injuries, reasons, and outcomes of pursuits. Bivariate analysis of pursuit characteristics and outcomes	33 % ended in an accident; 17 % ended with injury; over half initiated due to traffic violations, and many resulted in more serious charges; 68 % of suspects were apprehended for traffic violations and 48 % apprehended for felonies. Accidents more likely to occur when police proactively were "on the lookout"
Alpert and Dunham (1989)	Metro-Dade (FL) PD	1987	323		Examined the outcomes of pursuits, in particular whether they resulted in injury, damage, or arrest. Also examined characteristics of officers involved in pursuits	34 % resulted in an accident, but 55 % of pursuits did not result in serious injury, property damage, or a traffic accident; 73 % of pursuits resulted in arrest. Younger officers more likely to have negative outcomes
Alpert et al. (1996)	Omaha (NE) and Metro-Dade (FL) PDs, Aiken County (SC) Sheriff's Office	Metro-Dade: 1990–1994; Omaha: 1992–1994; Aiken County: 1993–1994	Metro-Dade: 1,049; Omaha: 229; Aiken County: 17		Descriptive and multi-variate statistical analysis of police pursuits; surveys law enforcement agencies about content of pursuit policies and effects of changes in policy on pursuit behavior	Changes in police pursuit policies led to either an increase in pursuits (when agencies changed from policies that were more restrictive to judgmental) or a decrease in pursuits (when agencies moved toward policies that are more restrictive). Accident as a proportion of pursuits: Metro-Dade = 41 %; Omaha = 32 %; Aiken County = 47 %. Proportion of pursuits that resulted in arrest: Metro-Dade = 75 %; Omaha = 52 %; Aiken County = 82 %

(continued)

Table 3.1 (continued)

Author(s) and year of study	Location of study	Years data were analyzed	Number pursuits studied	Other units studied	Brief summary	Key findings
Alpert et al. (1997)	Metro-Dade (FL)	1990–1994	1,049	255 officers and 51 inmates surveyed	Examined pursuits and use of force by officers after a high-speed vehicular pursuit and interviewed suspects of pursuits. Collected data in Metro-Dade, Omaha, and Aiken County	Of 1,049 reported pursuits, 33 % resulted in an accident, 74 % of pursuits resulted in an arrest, 45 % of arrests associated with an accident. 13 % of arrests involved use of force. Surveys found officers perceived excessive use of force was used sometimes during pursuits. 55 % of suspects interviewed reported excessive force
Alpert et al. (1997)	Omaha (NE)	1992–1994	229	491 officers and 38 inmates surveyed	Examined pursuits and use of force by officers after a high-speed pursuit, interviewing suspects of pursuits. Collected data in Metro-Dade, Omaha, and Aiken County	Of 229 reported pursuits, 52 % of pursuits resulted in arrest, 48 % of arrests associated with an accident. 36 % of arrests involved use of force. Surveys found officers perceived excessive use of force was used sometimes during pursuits. 43 % of suspects interviewed reported excessive force
Alpert et al. (1997)	Aiken County (SC)	1993–1994	17	52 officers and 32 inmates surveyed	Examined pursuits and use of force by officers after a high-speed vehicular pursuit and interviewed suspects of pursuits. Collected data in Metro-Dade, Omaha, and Aiken County	Of 17 reported pursuits, 47 % resulted in accidents, 82 % resulted in arrest, 57 % of those arrests associated with an accident. 3 % of arrests involved use of force. Surveys found officers perceived excessive use of force was used sometimes during pursuits. 34 % of suspects interviewed reported excessive force
Alpert (1988)	Baltimore City (MD)	1995–1996	89		Examines the use and outcomes of helicopters in police pursuits	Pursuits utilizing helicopters resulted in high arrest rates in Baltimore (83 %)
Alpert (1988)	Metro-Dade (FL) PDs	1995–1996	43		Examines the use and outcomes of helicopters in police pursuits	Pursuits utilizing helicopters resulted in high arrest rates in Miami (91 %)
Alpert et al. (2000)	Omaha (NE) and Metro-Dade (FL) PDs, Aiken County (SC) Sheriff's Office and Mesa (AZ)	1990–1994	1,295		Analyzed data on the nature, characteristics, and outcomes of police pursuits. This book also presents literature and legal updates and discussions from the original NIJ report	Update to the NIJ Final Report, referenced above as Alpert et al. (1996). Those who flee in vehicles do so regardless of high-speed pursuit; most who flee have not committed offenses customary of a full custodial arrest, serious offenders were a minority of who fled, and major discrepancy between police perception and that of offenders who initiated pursuits by fleeing

ACLU Found. of Southern California (1996)	California Highway Patrol	1993–1995	5,766		Analysis of accident, injury, and reason for pursuits	While 35–40 % of pursuits resulted in an accident or injury, only small proportion of the pursuits (between 5 % and 12 %) involved an individual suspected of a serious violent crime (most suspected of traffic and minor offenses)
Australian Institute of Criminology (2013)	Australia	2000–2011	Complete national data available 2009–2011; average 3,948.7 pursuits per year	218 deaths due to pursuits (2000–2011). 40 deaths from 2009–2011	Interested in fatalities as a result of pursuits, and reviews characteristics of pursuits that result in fatalities	185 fatal pursuit-related crashes resulting in 218 deaths. 62 % of deaths were alleged offenders. 38 % were noninvolved/innocent persons. Overall decline in crashes across 12 years and fewer deaths. Regional differences in terms of number of pursuits and fatalities. The most prevalent offense resulting in fatality was traffic related (38 %) followed by motor vehicle theft (31 %) and drink-driving (19 %)
Auten (1991)	86 agencies in Illinois	1990	286		Analysis of accidents, injuries, reasons for, and outcomes of pursuits	Most pursuits did not lead to injury or accident and were not initiated for suspected felonies (most were initiated from traffic violations). The majority of suspects were apprehended
Bayless and Osborne (1998)	California Highway Patrol	1994–1996	20,378	419 CEOs of agencies surveyed	Examined pursuit data provided by California Highway Patrol and also surveyed 419 chief executive officers of law enforcement agencies regarding police pursuit policies and concerns	Surveys indicated that 97 % had policies for pursuits, and 85 % required supervisory control of pursuits. 23 % indicated no training on pursuit policy had been provided. Regarding pursuit data, 26 % of pursuits resulted in collisions. Of the pursuits that resulted in collision, over 50 % occurred within 1–2 min of the pursuit, 73 % within 1–4 min, and 83 % of collisions occurred within 6 min of the pursuit
Beckman (1985) as reported in Charles et al. (1992) and Nugent et al. (1990)	75 agencies	1984	424	Surveyed officers in a follow-up study	Using 40 city police and 34 sheriff's departments plus Guam and the Virgin Islands, 424 pursuits were collected for analysis	12 % resulted in injury or death of suspect; no pedestrians injured, but 17 innocent third party motorists were injured, and 2 killed. 77 % of the suspects were captured. Property damage resulted in every 4.73 pursuits
Best and Eves (2004)	Wales, United Kingdom	2002–2003	344		Examined characteristics of officers involved (in particular their training) in relation to outcomes of pursuits	Only descriptive statistics provided; 23 % of incidents resulted in accidents, 40 % resulted in arrest

(continued)

Table 3.1 (continued)

Author(s) and year of study	Location of study	Years data were analyzed	Number pursuits studied	Other units studied	Brief summary	Key findings
Best and Eves (2005)	England and Wales, United Kingdom	1998–2001	64		Examined reports of post-incident management of police pursuits for disciplinary responses by agency and supervisors	Found that for 48 (76 %) of the cases, no disciplinary action or policy recommendation was made
Brewer and McGrath (1991)	Adelaide, Australia	1987–1988	143	38 randomly selected offenders	Analyzed pursuits and then examined a random selection ($n=38$) of offenders involved in the pursuits to determine demographic and criminal history characteristics of individuals involved in pursuits	Those at high risk for engaging in police pursuits are similar to those considered high-risk drivers generally (young, male, unlicensed, high blood-alcohol content). 96 % of recorded pursuits started with a traffic violation. 4.9 % resulted in an accident, and there was an 80 % apprehension rate
California Highway Patrol (1983)	State of California, and 10 agencies	1982	683		Examines characteristics and outcomes of police pursuits	29 % end in accidents, 11 % in injuries, 77 % arrest rate. Felony pursuits tend to result in more accidents than non-felony pursuits. Reviewed by Alpert and Anderson (1986) and Charles et al. (1992)
California Highway Patrol (2011)	State of California, multiple agencies pursuant to law requiring reporting	2010	5,024		Examines characteristics and outcomes of police pursuits for 2010, especially focused on California Highway Patrol (CHP) statistics	Of all pursuits, 30 % (1,508) resulted in a collision. Of the reported collisions, 64 % (967) were noninjury, 34 % (511) were injury, with 30 of these as fatal injury (2 %). In the 511 injury collisions, 766 persons were injured, 21 % were uninvolved third parties. The report also provides specific numbers for the CHP. 71 % apprehended. Apprehension rates vary by how the pursuit ends, with greatest apprehension for voluntary stops
Charles et al. (1992) and Falcone et al. (1992)	Illinois	1991	149	784 officers surveyed	Reviews past studies and conducts one additional empirical study (reported here). Conducts one empirical study of police pursuits and officer perceptions of pursuits in Volume II (reported here)	Vehicle pursuits are short (median is 5 min and about 3.2 miles). 14 % were initiated for felonies. Only 3 % were initiated by calls for service. 26 % resulted in accidents. 9 % resulted in injuries. Survey data revealed substantially more pursuits take place than official records indicate. Perceptions of pursuit causes often not aligned with reporting

Study	Location	Years	N	Focus	Findings
Crew (1992)	Houston (TX) PD	1987–1988	1,584	Evaluates the effects of pursuit policy on outcomes	After the policy went into effect, the reporting of police pursuits dropped 40 %
Crew and Hart (1999)	Minnesota Department of Public Safety	1989–1996	6,773	Conducts a cost–benefit analysis of police pursuits by comparing negative (accidents, injuries, damage) to positive (arrest, deterrence) outcomes of pursuits	The authors report two different accident statistics: 41 % of all pursuits in which an accident *occurred*, and 32 % of the pursuits which *ended* in an accident. 77 % of pursuits resulted in arrest. The researchers found a 60:1 benefit to cost ratio for police pursuits, although also note that the odds of a negative outcome of a pursuit are fairly high (30 %)
Criminal Justice Commission (1998)	Queensland PD, Australia	1992–1993; 1996–1997	63	Descriptive statistics on the nature, character, and outcome of pursuits which had ended in injury or death	A number of descriptive statistics are provided about these pursuits. Some highlighted findings were that pursued drivers tended to be male, often were unlicensed or influenced by alcohol. Study included breakdown of type of accidents as a result of pursuits. Single car accidents were the most frequent (57.1 %). 90 % of fleeing suspects were apprehended
Docking et al. (2007)	London	2004–2006	102	Descriptive statistics of road traffic incidents, including police pursuits - reasons, outcomes, and officer and suspect characteristics	Pursuit drivers tend to be young, male, uninsured, and disqualified from driving; 25 % of fleeing drivers were fatally injured; 50 % of fleeing drivers were seriously injured; 60 % of fleeing drivers were over the legal limit for alcohol consumption; incident reports were not completed consistently. Out of the 259 people (police not included) involved in the 102 incidents, 18 % were killed, 44 % seriously injured, and 38 % minor or no injuries. Most common reason for pursuit was reckless driving. 56 % of pursuits resulted in prosecution
Dunham and Alpert (1991)	Metro-Dade (FL) PD	1987	323	Examines the correlation between officer age and gender and police pursuits	There were gender and age differences in pursuits—females were more cautious but were just as likely to apprehend suspects with less negative outcomes. Younger officers tended to have more negative outcomes. 73 % end in arrest, 34 % result in accidents, and 23 % result in injuries

(continued)

Table 3.1 (continued)

Author(s) and year of study	Location of study	Years data were analyzed	Number pursuits studied	Other units studied	Brief summary	Key findings
Dunham et al. (1998)	Miami (FL), Omaha (NE) and Lexington and Richland counties (SC)	1994	146		Interviewed jail inmates recently involved in pursuits to discover what factors might contribute to a suspect having a higher risk of engaging the police in a vehicular pursuit	Previous chase experience, thoughts of punishment, safety, and driving under the influence increased the odds of engaging the police in a pursuit. However, these factors did not affect the final outcome of the pursuit. 30 % of pursuits resulted in accidents, 65 % resulted in apprehension
Fennessy et al. (1970)	N. Carolina HP, Fairfax County (VA), Bloomington (IL) and South Bend (IN) PDs	circa 1970	46		Broad study of the police pursuit law and policies, including descriptions of the number of police pursuits and their consequences/risks	80 % ended in successful apprehension of the offender. 11 % ended in a crash. Most injuries are incurred by individuals other than the police. Over 90 % of pursuits are initiated from traffic-related offenses. Some risk factors found were alcohol, drivers license status (14 % of fleeing suspects did not have license), and youth. See also Fennessy and Joscelyn (1972). Study emphasizes the difficulty in obtaining historical data about pursuits
Hannigan (1995)	California Highway Patrol and multiple California agencies	1993–1995	over 5,000		Examines the reason and the outcome of pursuits. Because the report could not be located, it is unclear exactly how many pursuits were studied	Summaries indicate that while about half of the pursuits began as minor traffic violations; if apprehended, 73 % resulted in felony arrest. As already mentioned, no more information on this report could be located
Hoffman (2003)	Queensland, Australia	2000–2002 for main database (STS); 2001–2002 (ESC files); 1997–2001 (CMC)	1,259 (STS); 34 (ESC); 66 (CMC)		Three databases used. Examines the reason why pursuits were initiated and the outcome of pursuits in terms of injuries, arrests, and charges. Also looks at characteristics of the pursued driver	The most common reason given for pursuits was traffic offenses. 29 % of pursuits resulted in injury. Over 90 % were males and 3/4 were under 30 years old. According to Crime and Misconduct Commission (CMC; 2011) data, 46 % of pursued drivers were not licensed. CMC data showed injuries to 43 % of pursued drivers, 34 % pursued passengers, 14 % police officers, and 9 % third-party vehicles. STS data showed 29 % of pursuits involved collisions, most commonly (60 %) a single-vehicle accident. According to STS, 46 % of pursuits were abandoned

Study	Location	Year	Sample		Description	Findings
Homel (1990)	Perth, Australia	1990	346		Describes the outcomes of these pursuits	51 % of pursuits resulted in an apprehension, 34 % of pursuits resulted in crashes, and almost 7 % resulted in death. Most apprehended individuals were charged with car theft (70 %), while the rest with other traffic offenses
Hutson et al. (2007)	United States	1982–2004	Only pursuits that resulted in fatalities were studied.	6,336 total fatal crashes from police pursuits	Examines fatal crashes resulting from police pursuits from the National Highway Traffic Safety Administration (NHTSA) FARS database	6,336 fatal pursuit-related crashes resulted in 7,430 fatalities (1.2 fatalities per crash). 70.5 % of deaths were drivers of the chased vehicle. 27 % of deaths were uninvolved individuals. Various statistics are given by year and state. Largest frequency of deaths a result of collision with a moving vehicle (38 %)
Lawler (2013)	Milwaukee (MN)	2012	63		Examined all pursuits in Milwaukee PD within a year. Also examined trends of pursuits since advent of new felony-only policy in 2010	Pursuits declined by 77 % since 2002, with large declines after implementation of 2010 policy. 38.7 % resulted in a crash or accident, one with bystander. 6 % resulted in an injury. 45 % of pursuits were terminated by law enforcement, many did not meet criteria
Lucadamo (1994)	Baltimore County (MD) PD	1987–1993	1,064		Examines the correlates of pursuits that did not result in a crash or collision	Found that years of service, weather, number of police vehicles, and entering another jurisdiction could accurately predict 92 % of the pursuits that did not result in accidents and 65 % of all pursuit outcomes
Lum and Fachner (2008)	IACP Pursuits Database (multiple agencies)	2001–2007	7,737		Examined data in the IACP pursuits database, which includes voluntary pursuit reports from 56 agencies across 30 states	Pursuits primarily initiated because traffic violation (42 %) or the car was believed to be stolen (18 %). 24 % resulted in accident. Common conditions that lead to accidents include ice, the suspect not being licensed, and heavier traffic. Other conditions and characteristics of pursuits are examined

(continued)

Table 3.1 (continued)

Author(s) and year of study	Location of study	Years data were analyzed	Number pursuits studied	Other units studied	Brief summary	Key findings
Nelson and Brune (1991) as reported in Charles et al. (1992)	Chicago Police Department	1988–1990	3,041		Reporters for the *Chicago Sun Times* examined Chicago PD files, court records, and interviewed police, witnesses, suspects	32 % of pursuits reported ending in an accident, and 8 % resulted in injury. In other data collection, it was found that police may underreport chases as well as injuries; officers receive minimal training, and department rules may be ineffective. 71 % resulted in arrest
Oechsli (1992)	Kentucky State Police	1989–1991	510		Analyzed nature, characteristics, and outcomes of police pursuits, including accidents	41 % of the pursuits were initiated by traffic violations. 53 % were due to an alcohol or drug violation. 25 % of the individuals pursued had an invalid license, and 3 % of these drivers were using a stolen vehicle. 22 % of pursuits ended in accidents; 5 % ended in injuries. 77 % of pursuits resulted in apprehension
O'Keefe (1989)	Houston PD	1988–1988	316		Examined descriptive data such as day of week, suspect information, and road or surface conditions, and operational data such as the mean age and patrol experience of the involved officer, events ending in pursuit, and injuries sustained	The mean age of officers involved in pursuits was 29, with 6 years of experience. Pursuit distances averaged 5 miles with a mean maximum speed of 66 mph. 80 % of suspects who fled from police were arrested. 63 % of pursuits originated from class c traffic stops or violations (typical offenses). There were no officer injuries or deaths
Payne and Fenske (1997)	Michigan State Police	1991–1992	197		Examined lighting conditions under which pursuits occurred and compares police accidents that resulted from pursuits and those resulting from other incidents in different light conditions	Pursuit accidents and fatality rate are significantly higher during darkness than nonpursuit accidents/fatalities, although other injury accidents were more likely to occur during daylight or darkness rather than dusk and dawn conditions. 33 % resulted in accidents

Study	Location	Date	Sample	Description	Findings
Patinkin and Bingham (1986) as reported in Charles et al. (1992)	Chicago Police Department	1984–1985	741	Study of pursuits after policy was initiated in 1984 by police chief	76 % resulted in arrest. Pursuits were terminated in 11 % of the cases, and 5 % personal injuries reported. 18 % of pursuits ended in some kind of accident. *Note*: Hicks reports this differently—as 24 % accident rate
Rivara and Mack (2004)	United States	1994–2002	2,654 fatal crashes due to pursuits were analyzed	Analyzed information from the Fatality Analysis Reporting and the Crashworthiness Data Systems of the National Highway Traffic Safety Administration regarding police motor vehicle crashes that resulted in fatalities	2,654 fatal crashes involving 3,965 vehicles and 3,146 fatalities were recorded, of which 1,088 were individuals not in the fleeing vehicle. Crashes occurred during the night, on local roads, and at high speeds. Most pursued drivers had prior motor vehicle convictions
Senese and Lucadamo (1996)	unidentified	September 1985–January 1992	1,064	Examined the nature, characteristics, and outcome of police pursuits, and also looked at correlates of police pursuits that resulted in accidents	About 1/3 (37 %) of all pursuits ended in an accident. Less experienced officers had nearly the same proportion of pursuits ending in accidents as the more experienced officers. Influential variables differentiating pursuits that ended in accidents were: weather, number of police units involved, reason for pursuit, time of day, lighting, road conditions, and type of roadway
Victoria Police Service (2012)	Victoria, Australia	2002–2011	6,061 pursuits and 1,703 terminations	Examines trends in pursuits and terminations in Victoria, Australia	Approximately 10 % of pursuits result in collision, with an increase from 2002 to 2011. Pursuits have increased annually since 2002, as have self-terminations. A total of 27 fatalities have resulted. This analysis also reviewed pursuit policy by Victoria police and compliance by officers
Wells and Falcone (1997)	Illinois	1993–1995	197	Compares ISPERN pursuit data set to previously reported data sets	Fairly high convergence among various studies and data sources for typical characteristics of police pursuits despite variations in data collection efforts and variables. 18 % of pursuits resulted in an accident, while 62 % resulted in arrest

suspect, blood alcohol content of the fleeing suspect) have also been examined (see, e.g., Alpert and Dunham 1990; Brewer and McGrath 1991; Dunham and Alpert 1991; Dunham et al. 1998; Hoffman 2003), although less frequently and sometimes only using estimations (especially regarding fleeing suspect characteristics). Although we did not find systematic discussions about the race and ethnicity of officers and suspects involved in pursuits, there were some exceptions (see Alpert and Dunham 1990; Dunham et al. 1998).[2]

Most consistently, the studies in Table 3.1 report on the negative outcomes (rates of crashes, injuries, and deaths) or pursuits and also their possible benefits (usually measured by rate of apprehensions). Thirty-one studies reported sufficient information to calculate the proportion of pursuits that resulted in a crash. The average is approximately 30 % (SD 10.5 %, minimum = 5 %, maximum = 38 %). Twenty-eight studies reported enough information to calculate the percentage of pursuits resulting in arrest. For those studies, the average arrest rate is approximately 72 % of pursuits (SD 11.95 %, minimum = 40 %, maximum = 91 %).[3]

We should be cautious about the results of these studies as with any research using official data. Pursuits reported by law enforcement may not be representative of the population of pursuits (for reasons discussed below). Reports may be generated because a crash occurred, an arrest was made, or because the pursuit was not terminated immediately. Interestingly, the averages of the studies are similar to the most recent California Highway Patrol (CHP) report (2011). California law since 2006 has required law enforcement agencies in California to report police pursuits within 30 days of occurrence. In the CHP's 2010 data, 30 % of approximately 5,024 pursuits resulted in a collision, while 71 % of pursuits resulted in apprehension.

These summary statistics on negative outcomes, costs, and benefits provide an important challenge to agencies thinking about using pursuits as a routine operational tactic. On the one hand, the research provides a warning to those making legal decisions about police pursuits like the one in *Scott v. Harris*. Specifically, the research strongly suggests that crashes occur in at least 30 % of pursuits. Even if the police will not be held legally responsible for the outcome of pursuits, the research points to a real public safety concern about them. At the same time, there appears to be a high probability of apprehension after a pursuit. Indeed, Crew and Hart (1999) interpreted findings of low rates of collisions/injuries to high rates of arrest as a benefit-to-cost ratio of 60:1 (they also report that the odds of a negative outcome are 30 %).

However, upon closer examination of the research, the benefits gained from apprehension of fleeing individuals may be less salient. Studies show that the probability of apprehension is not equal across all pursuits. Rather, the probability of apprehension is highest when individuals voluntarily stop. Certainly, the probability of apprehension without injury or crash is very high for voluntarily stops versus apprehensions as a result of a crash or use of countermeasures.

---

[2] The IACP pursuit database does provide the opportunity for agencies to submit this information to the database.

[3] These include apprehensions after a crash.

Further, we still know little about the differences between individuals who choose to flee from the police and those who do not. There is some evidence that individuals who flee have prior criminal histories that include violent offenses (see Brewer and McGrath 1991). However, Dunham et al. (1998) interviewed offenders who had fled from the police and found that the most common reason given for fleeing in a vehicle was that the car was stolen (32 % of the offenders provided this as one of the reasons they fled). The research also indicates that the initiating offense for many pursuits is a traffic violation, not a violent crime (see, e.g., American Civil Liberties Union Foundation of Southern California 1996; Hoffman 2003). However, research indicates that the initiating event differs significantly from charges that are later brought against apprehended drivers. In other words, while most of the studies report that the initial offense for a pursuit was traffic related or for some other minor infraction, the final charge for a suspect was often more severe (see Alpert 1987; Hannigan 1995; Lucadamo 1994; Nugent et al. 1990). It would also be important to determine whether these charges are related to the driving behavior of the suspect during the pursuit (e.g., assault with a deadly weapon using a vehicle). The meaning of findings regarding the potential benefits of pursuits needs further exploration.

The empirical research on pursuits focuses much more on understanding the nature, characteristics, and outcomes of pursuits, but pays minimal attention to the impact of policies or supervision on the outcomes of pursuits. Thus, even if calculations of costs and benefits of pursuits could be estimated, researchers would then need to determine whether changes in policies could significantly affect such measures.[4] For example, can alternative strategies (helicopters, use of license plate readers, delayed investigations, stopping devices) change the cost–benefit calculation of pursuits? Does implementing a more restrictive pursuit policy in fact reduce the number of crashes, injuries, and related costs of pursuits? Do restrictive policies lead to more (or fewer) voluntary stops by fleeing suspects or differences in case clearance rates?

There is little evidence that more individuals will flee, that crime rates will increase, or that case clearances will decline if an agency adopts more restrictive pursuit policies (or even "no-pursuit" policies). Indeed, crime clearances have stayed relatively stable over time despite agencies adopting policies that are more restrictive. What may matter more in determining what makes offenders flee, therefore, is not an offender's prior felony history or the agency's pursuit policies, but rather the *perceived* seriousness of the current situation in which offenders find themselves or the series of interactions between the officer and the individual. As Alpert and Smith (2008) point out, even within a more lenient legal environment, agencies may not change their pursuit policies to be less restrictive because they perceive no significant improvement in the benefits they might obtain from increased arrest rates. They may still feel that the injuries, liabilities, and reduced support from the community are serious enough costs to justify strict pursuit policies.

---

[4]One reviewer also suggested that, "It may also be useful to examine the aggregate liability costs related to civil judgments involving police pursuits."

Thus, improving the evidence base for pursuits not only requires a greater understanding of the characteristics and conditions of pursuits as linked to specific outcomes, but also the impact that policies, practices, and interventions have on those same outcomes. Has either research or case law affected policies? We now turn to this question in the next chapter.

Chapter 4
The Impact of Research on Pursuit Policies

The central concern of this monograph is whether the four decades of research on police pursuits have had much impact on legal decisions and law enforcement policy. What primarily influences police decisions about pursuits and how might research play a more important role in the development of pursuit policies? In this chapter, we first discuss the state of pursuit policies and then explore the impact that research as well as the legal analysis may have had on them.

Pursuit Policies

Understanding pursuit policies, what drives them, and how changes in policies affect outcomes has been subjected to even less empirical scrutiny and research than police pursuits themselves. Fennessy et al. conducted one of the earliest examinations of pursuit policies in 1970 (see also Fennessy and Joscelyn 1972). In their study, they requested policies from 130 US city agencies and 48 state agencies. The researchers received policies from 52 of the cities and 22 of the states, from which they identified three types of policies: "Officer Judgment," "Restrictive," and "Pursuits Discouraged."[1] In the 1970s, the "Officer Judgment" model appeared to be the most frequent type of policy in police agencies. Fennessy et al. also reported that very few agencies regularly and systematically recorded pursuit data, and they were not able to obtain any archived data on pursuits from any of the agencies in their study.

---

[1] Fennessy and Joscelyn (1972) define the officer judgment model as "All basic decisions to initiate, conduct, or terminate hot pursuit are made by the street officer. His decisions are subject to internal review and possible legal action, depending on "due care" provisions." They define the restrictive policy model as, "There are certain restrictions on the officer's decision to initiate, conduct, or terminate a pursuit. Examples are: only pursue for felonies; no speed above 20 mph over posted limits; stop at intersections. They define pursuits discouraged model as "Officers are cautioned or discouraged from engaging in hot pursuit. None of the agencies, however, expressly forbids pursuit if there is no other choice and if it is an extreme emergency." (pp. 394–395)

G.P. Alpert and C. Lum, *Police Pursuit Driving: Policy and Research*, SpringerBriefs in Criminology, DOI 10.1007/978-1-4939-0712-0_4, © The Author(s) 2014

Nugent et al. (1990) examined pursuit policies in four agencies that had restrictive policies—Nassau County, New York; St. Petersburg, Florida; Mesa, Arizona; and Phoenix, Arizona. Even within a restrictive environment, Nugent and colleagues discovered various similarities as well as differences across policies regarding radio communications during pursuits, termination of pursuits, the use of techniques such as boxing-in, ramming, and roadblocks, rules about the use of firearms during a pursuit, alternatives to pursuits, interjurisdictional rules, supervisory roles, and review procedures. From their analysis, they noted that four major elements appeared to constitute these pursuit policies: (1) a specific pursuit directive, (2) training, (3) alternatives to high-speed pursuits, and (4) a review process. They also attempted to measure the number of pursuits before and after policies were implemented, although were unable to successfully discern the meaning of numerical changes in pursuits.

Research by Alpert and his colleagues (1996; see also Alpert et al. 2000; Kenney and Alpert 1997) comprehensively examined pursuit policy using a national survey of 436 police agencies in the United States. The survey asked agencies about general characteristics of their organizations, the type of pursuit policy they followed, whether they recorded pursuit activities, supervisory control, and disciplinary procedures of pursuits, the methods they used to stop fleeing vehicles, and litigation experiences. They found (as reported in Chap. 4 of Alpert et al. 1996 and Chap. 2 of Alpert et al. 2000):

- 91 % of agencies reported having a written policy governing police pursuits
- 48 % of the agencies had modified their policies within the 2 years prior to the study
- 87 % of recently modified policies were made more restrictive
- 48 % of the agencies reported allowing pursuits for any offense, while 16 % reported pursuits were only allowed for felony offenses
- 58 % of agencies only allowed marked cars to engage in pursuit
- 11 % limited the maximum speed of the pursuing vehicle
- 40 % of agencies required the pursuit to end when the suspect had been identified
- Municipal agencies were more likely to impose supervisory control, limit pursuits to felonies, and limit pursuits to marked vehicles only
- Roadblocks were the most frequently reported alternative method of stopping vehicles (42 %); ramming, immobilization, and portable barrier strips were rarely permitted
- 31 % of agencies maintained police pursuit statistics or data systematically
- Municipal and larger agencies were more likely to collect pursuit data

In 1997, the Pursuit Management Task Force (PMTF) surveyed 1,420 agencies about their pursuit policies, of which 419 responded (Bayless and Osborne 1998). The PMTF found (pp. 7–9):

- 99 % of responding agencies allowed their officers to pursue vehicles
- 97 % had written policies regarding pursuits
- 85 % of pursuit policies required supervisory control

- 41 % allowed the use of tire deflation devices; these devices were also most often noted as efficient
- 50 % of agencies allowed officers to use one of the following: ramming, boxing-in, or channeling techniques to stop vehicles (35 % of policies allowed ramming, 29 % allowed the use of boxing-in as a pursuit-ending technique, 25 % allowed the use of barricading)
- 3 % of agencies allowed for the use of "PIT" maneuvers[2]
- 25 % of agencies were aware of pursuit technologies, but chose not to use them for various reasons, including cost, availability, potential liability, and a lack of knowledge on the effectiveness of such technologies

Other studies added to the knowledge about pursuit policies. Sharp (2003) examined the policies of 30 agencies finding that many limited the number and type of police vehicles that could be involved, but that in almost a third of the agencies, officers still had discretion in whether to pursue fleeing suspects, and that nonviolent felony suspects could be pursued. In an examination of only state-level agencies, Hicks (2006) found policies to have both administrative and operational elements in policies. Administrative elements related to bureaucratic operations, such as record keeping, report writing, definitions, and safety, while operational elements emphasized officer conduct such as speed, shooting from the vehicle, "boxing-in," off road pursuits, and caravanning.[3] Hicks found that while many administrative elements were found in the majority of pursuit policies, some were more prominent than others. Policy elements such as safety, pursuit restrictions, offense seriousness, report writing, and the use of caravanning, unmarked cars, or termination were often mentioned. Less pronounced across policies were elements specifying the authority to pursue, intentional collisions, shooting from vehicles, speed, or the use of air support and tire-deflation devices.

Recently, Lum and Fachner (2008) conducted a content analysis on pursuit policies collected from a stratified random sample of police agencies in 2007. They used Question 57 from the 2003 *Law Enforcement Management and Administration Survey* or "LEMAS" (see US Department of Justice, Bureau of Justice Statistics 2006) to identify agencies with different types of pursuit policies from which to conduct a stratified sample (at that time, only the 2003 LEMAS data were available). The question asked was, "Which of the following best describes your agency's written policy for pursuit driving?" Choices included *discouragement*, which LEMAS describes as "discouraging all pursuits," *judgmental*, described as "leaves decisions to officer's discretion," *restrictive* as "restricts decisions of officers to specific criteria such as type of offense, speed, etc.," and *other*.

There were 2,859 agencies that responded to the 2003 LEMAS, and 99.8 % answered this question. At the time of the 2003 LEMAS, the majority of agencies

---

[2] "PIT" or Pursuit Intervention Technique refers to maneuvers in which the pursuing vehicle makes contact with the rear side panel of the fleeing vehicle, pushing through it and causing it to spin out, or lose control, in the hope that the fleeing driver will stop.

[3] Caravanning typically refers to three or more police vehicles aligning themselves in a pursuit. Some policies allow for three vehicles to pursue fleeing suspects but prohibit caravanning.

described their policies as restrictive (67 %) rather than judgmental (23 %), discouraging (5 %), or other (3 %). The agencies with 100 or more officers reported restrictive policies (73 %) more frequently than agencies with fewer than 100 officers (64 %).[4] Lum and Fachner randomly selected 25 agencies from each category (restrictive, judgmental, discouraging, or other) and requested their pursuit policy for a detailed examination. In total, 77 of the 100 agencies responded (US Department of Justice, Bureau of Justice Statistics 2007).

In their content analysis, they examined 27 components of pursuit policies, including whether pursuits were allowed, aspects of supervision, communication, officer safety, techniques used, whether pursuits were recorded, whether policies included guidance about different road, weather, traffic, and environmental conditions, and whether rules were included about unmarked cars, motorcycles, use of force, and the information on the offense and offender. We reproduce Lum and Fachner's results in Table 4.2 to show some common themes that emerged from examining the content of the pursuit policies.

Many agencies required the recording of pursuits and were aware of public safety concerns related to pursuits. Interestingly, policies appeared much less focused on suspect safety, although Lum and Fachner (2008) in the same report found that over 65 % of those injured from recorded pursuits in the International Association of Chiefs of Police pursuit database were suspects. Although visibility, weather, speed, and traffic conditions were also found as possible factors influencing the probability of injury in not only Lum and Fachner's report but others before it, most policies indicated these decisions were left to the discretion of officers. And, certain devices, such as tire deflation and roadblocks, were used more than paralleling or intentional collision. However, no rigorous outcome evaluation exists as to whether these tactics are cost-beneficial and cost-effective.

Pursuit policies, as with standard operating procedures and policies of law enforcement more generally, also contain very little educational information about pursuits, or even citations to research or statistical knowledge that informed the policy's development. Thus, we can only guess how much policy is actually influenced by research knowledge or even an agency's internal data collection. Often, law enforcement procedures and policies are based in legal reasoning, "insider knowledge" (see Cullen et al. 2009), best practices, experience, and traditions, not in research or an agency's data (Lum 2009; Sherman 1998). Further, the training related to a particular policy is often conducted in academies through the memorization of policies and procedures, rather than the understanding of the knowledge base or reasoning behind them. The interaction between research, policy development, and policy implementation in policing is still vague, and likely tenuous.

---

[4] More recently, the 2007 LEMAS included a new category in its pursuits question: "Prohibition (prohibits all pursuits)" in Question 46. However, the resulting data from this question is not publicly available. In correspondence with the Bureau of Justice Statistics on July 13, 2013, officials responded to the authors' inquiry regarding data for Question 46 stating that "There was an error in the wording of the pursuit policy question which affected the responses and resulted in the data not being valid. Therefore, the question was excluded from the archived data." While it is likely that the trend towards more restrictive policies continues, we are uncertain given that the data are unavailable.

Table 4.2 Common
themes of pursuit policies

1. Supervision, monitoring, and accountability	%
Prior supervisor authorization needed	1.4
Supervisor is responsible for termination	52.1
Communication	84.9
Pursuits recorded	89.0
2. Safety	**%**
Suspect safety specifically mentioned	34.2
Officer safety specifically mentioned	84.9
Public safety specifically mentioned	95.9
3. Driving conditions	**%**
Limits placed on officer speed	4.1
Off road pursuits permitted	5.5
Driving the wrong way is permitted	19.2
Visibility considerations are discretionary	57.5
Weather considerations are discretionary	91.8
Traffic considerations are discretionary	91.8
4. Vehicles involved	**%**
Motorcycles cannot be used	11.0
Unmarked cars cannot be used	15.1
Any mention of air assistance	28.8
Motorcycles can be used until marked car is available	53.4
Unmarked cars can be used until marked car available	54.8
More than one vehicle can pursue	84.9
5. Situational context	**%**
Suspect identification must end the pursuit	4.1
Limits pursuits by offense types	47.9
6. Devices and tactics	**%**
Paralleling could be used	32.9
Intentional collision could be used	57.5
Any contact is considered "deadly force"	60.3
Roadblocks could be used	61.6
Tire deflation could be used	61.6

Reproduced from Lum and Fachner (2008, p. 40)

Not only are we uncertain about the impact that the research shown in Chap. 3 has on pursuit policies (or legal cases that also may shape policy), there has been no rigorous evaluation that we know of which examines the impact of changes in pursuit policies or the use of pursuit technologies and tactics on desired outcomes such as crime control, public safety, apprehension, or case clearance. As already mentioned, roadblocks and tire deflation seem to be popular methods to stop pursuits, but they continue to be unevaluated in terms of effectiveness compared with alternative methods. We also don't know if terminated pursuits are likely to result in the apprehension of the fleeing suspect anyway, through other investigative means. Another important research question is whether more use of supervisor authorization would reduce crashes. As Lum and Fachner argue, "it may be that in the moment prior to when an officer decides to engage in a pursuit, this may be the most opportune point where a knowledgeable and less-stressed third party or supervisor might be able to exercise the greatest control over a future outcome" (p. 41). This hypothesis remains untested. Examining the relationship between discontinuing a pursuit and officer judgment might also help understand pursuit outcomes.

More understanding about the context and environment of pursuits is also needed to determine whether policy statements about these factors are evidence based. For example, should exceptions be made to pursuit allowances during the night or in inclement weather? Should there be different allowances for pursuits in densely populated areas versus more rural locations? Can supervisors who make decisions to restrict pursuits be trained on this knowledge to make more calculated decisions about the potential costs of any given pursuit?

Finally, as discussed in Chap. 1, research indicates that police can be much more effective when they proactively target and use tailored and specific strategies at selected places (Lum et al. 2011b; Weisburd and Eck 2004). However, this proactive targeting also presents an interesting challenge to the management of pursuits. Proactive targeting at high crime locations may create situations in which officers have an increased rate of encountering individuals who flee from them. Perhaps agencies should strategize not only about what police should do when they conduct targeted, focused deterrence efforts in crime hot spots, but also strategize about how to prevent suspects from fleeing. And if a suspect does flee, plans for targeted areas should include a response to the fleeing vehicle.

What Influences Change?

While research efforts on pursuits have increased considerably and empirical knowledge has improved dramatically in the last few decades, its impact on changes in pursuit policies remains unclear. As with many areas of policing, research on pursuits has not always been translated into practice. There are many barriers to law enforcement being receptive to research and crime analysis and even more that prohibit this information from becoming institutionalized into everyday policing systems (Lum et al. 2012). Sadly, the data do not always convince managers to modify policies or even training. As we noted in Chap. 1, police pursuits have been a part of police history from the beginning. Further, many questions about pursuits and their management through policing policy remain unanswered, muddying our understanding of what might affect change in police pursuits policy over time. Why would some offenders ride off on their horses when others would give up and take their chances with the police or court system? Why would some of these officers take significant risks while others are more cautious? As we approach 2015, we still do not have a systematic understanding of the suspects who flee and the officers who chase. While we have learned a great deal from our research studies, especially those that have been replicated (see Alpert 1997), we know less about the influence of the agencies' "cultures" and "work environments" on their management of pursuits. Although our level of knowledge continues to grow, many police managers look to justifications other than the available evidence to authorize or prohibit pursuits.

In particular, police officers and managers continue to look to their colleagues for advice, "best practices," and consent concerning pursuits. It is not natural for police officers or supervisors to terminate the active pursuit of a fleeing suspect as they are often trained and conditioned to prioritize the apprehension of these suspects. Even when there are data that show the likely behavior of fleeing suspects and likely negative outcome of pursuits when continued, these officers hold on to the old adage that the police must apprehend suspects regardless of the risks to citizens, officers, or the suspects. Some officers and managers will continue chases at any cost and their colleagues might consider them "good" or "aggressive" (positively noted), or masters of their craft. Fortunately, in many agencies these beliefs have been replaced by more balanced approaches that are represented by policies and practices that weigh risks and rewards based on data and limit chases to serious and violent crimes. However, changing a policy and even reinforcing those modifications in training does not guarantee that an officer's attitudes or behavior will change. Many agencies throughout the country collect and maintain statistical data on pursuits. Some of these agencies even evaluate the data, publish them in annual reports,[5] and provide the outcomes. Although great progress has been made by many agencies, too many chases continue to violate policies and result in too many crashes, injuries, deaths, and financial and emotional costs.

Even when a chief or sheriff decides to change a policy, what is the impact to the officers? Unfortunately no systematic study has been conducted on the opinions and attitudes of officers in a wide variety of agencies over time, but what we know from single-site studies and the analysis of behavioral measures is that change takes time. For example, when the Metro-Dade (now Miami-Dade) Police Department changed from a vague, judgmental pursuit policy to a "violent felony only" policy in the early 1990s (Alpert 1997), the department initially struggled with this change. The police bargaining association complained to the administration, politicians, and the public that this change removed a valuable crime-fighting tactic. Many officers individually and collectively complained that it would obstruct real law enforcement. Many times when a supervisor would terminate a pursuit there were "chicken" noises made on the radio or officers would click their microphones to show displeasure.

However, the senior managers faced a dilemma: how to modify behavior that had been part of the agency since its beginning, but also maintain an officer's morale that often arises from his/her instinct to apprehend criminals. Their approach was the iron fist in a velvet glove. The pursuit training was changed from demonstrating how to chase to teaching the risks of chases by using the agency's own data, including crashes and injuries as well as stories of pursuits that had created public relations nightmares for the agency. Officers who had been in chases with negative outcomes helped with the training. There was a distinct attempt to change the way

---

[5] The Commission on Accreditation for Law Enforcement Agencies (CALEA) requires agencies to collect data and generate a report on their pursuit activates.

officers thought about pursuit through training, education, and supervision, to change this aspect of the culture of the agency, and to modify the behavior of the officers. The agency also employed a disciplinary process to help manage those officers who were not paying sufficient attention to the new policy and training.

The agency was able to reduce pursuits by approximately 80 % during the first year of the change and several pursuits that did occur were determined to be out-of-policy and generated disciplinary actions. While the agency leaders and politicians recognized the necessity of changing the policies and modifying training, efforts to survey officers on their attitudes and behavior were not well received. The commanders felt that any attempt to ask the officers would be detrimental to the changed efforts that were under way. It would have been interesting to have surveyed the officers before the changes, after the changes took place, and then after several years to determine the ways the changes influenced the officers' opinions as well as their behavior. This was a missed opportunity to find out how the officers reported the pursuits and if the reporting process had changed with the policy changes. To answer the question "Did research impact policy?," such studies need to be conducted.

Fast-forward a few decades since the policy modifications and the subsequent changes in culture and work environment. Compared to the 1990s, the Miami-Dade Police Department has changed. Pursuits are not the norm, most officers have never been in a pursuit, and officers are not seen as weak or ostracized when they terminate a pursuit. New recruits received new and data-driven training when they came on the force, which also reduced the pressure to chase. As officers became older, they were not as interested in pursuing at great risk as they were as young officers. However, the officers who were trained under the old policy and encouraged to chase aggressively even for minor offenses had the most difficult time adjusting to the new era. A review of the agency records showed most of the officers whose chases were out-of-policy had 5–10 years of experience and were academy trained and/or received field training that encouraged a pro-chase philosophy (Alpert et al. 2000). The change in Miami-Dade can likely be attributed to some combination of court decisions, political influences, agency performance data, and a progressive and strong management team that reformed the work environment and officer culture.

More recently, Milwaukee, Minnesota changed its pursuit policies in 2010 to allow pursuits only in situations where officers know or have probable cause that a violent felony has occurred or is about to occur (Barton 2013; Lawler 2013, footnote 2). The main reason reported by Barton (2013) of the *Journal Sentinel* for this change was the killing of four civilians during high speed chases in 2009 and 2010. Chief Flynn also suggested that officer concerns that dangerous criminals would escape did not materialize in MPD, stating that "… here in Milwaukee, the vast majority of people who choose to flee the police are fleeing for what turns out to be minor and foolish reasons" (which was also supported by Lawler 2013). Interestingly, in the case of Milwaukee, opposition to the restricted policy came initially from community groups and citizens, not from the police department.

Thus, many factors affect pursuit policies and practices in police agencies. While an evidence-based policing approach (see Lum 2009; Lum and Koper 2013; Madden and Alpert 1999; Sherman 1998) would require that both the pursuits research and analysis of an agency's own data should influence a chief executive's thinking towards adopting restrictive policies, this is not always the case. Sometimes risk managers and insurance companies that draft model policies and consider the costs also influence some departments. Other agencies are influenced by case law and other legal requirements, and still others by the multimillion dollar judgments that are handed down to victims and their families by juries and judges. And many police managers may still be guided by personal opinions or informal networks, some of whom have not made significant changes to their policies in years and continue to want officers to make their own decisions about risks and benefits based on insufficient training and supervision. However, as we saw in the Kentucky Supreme Court case (*Chambers v. Ideal Pure Milk Co.*, 1952), the causes of negative outcomes have been at least partially attributed to the actions of the police for more than 60 years. Regardless of blame or legal causes, it would be an interesting exercise to analyze the impact of a negative pursuit outcome on the attitudes of officers, managers, and the public and see what actions the chief or sheriff would take to avoid the outcry from citizens and politicians.

Perhaps the impact would be even greater if a prominent citizen or politician were injured or killed in a pursuit. There may be local examples of pursuits that have injured or killed prominent citizens, but the impact of one tragic pursuit made pursuits a national issue. In 1992, then Congressman Byron Dorgan, a Democrat from North Dakota, whose mother was killed as a result of a police pursuit of a drunk driver, introduced the National Pursuit Awareness Act. The Act provided funding for the Federal Law Enforcement Training Center to develop guidelines and provide training to state and local law enforcement agencies and officers throughout the country and was an impetus for critical discussions about pursuits in the United States. There were Congressional hearings on pursuits and many state legislatures followed the lead and held their own hearings to understand the role of pursuits in law enforcement. In some instances, state and local law and regulations were developed as a means to guide pursuits (e.g., New Jersey, California).

In a world where decisions are driven by data and evidence, pursuits would be restricted and used as a tactic only for the most serious offenders. However, the world of law enforcement is influenced not only by evidence, but also by history, organizational culture, law enforcement traditions, old-fashioned mindsets, "best" practices, and politics. The pursuit pendulum continues to swing, moving in one direction or the other depending on whose influential voice is speaking and how the justifications for pursuits are expressed.

Chapter 5
The Future of Police Pursuits Research and Policy

Police pursuits have been a controversial topic for more than 40 years. What law enforcement and even the public initially understood as a necessary function is now viewed as a dangerous tactic that is appropriate under very limited circumstances. Any analysis of a pursuit must involve balancing two competing interests—the need to apprehend a fleeing suspect and the risks to the public, officer, and suspect. How the police and the public determine the appropriate balance influences the way police manage pursuit driving, and how the organizational culture of the police is altered. Pursuit-related research can help interpret the costs, benefits, and consequences of this balancing act, and if translated to practice can have an impact on the policies and decisions associated with police pursuits.

Our examination of legal cases and empirical research has led us to several conclusions and recommendations for law enforcement as well as for the future of research on pursuit driving. Before we turn to specific suggestions, we review the findings about pursuits that help frame our recommendations.

What Have We Learned?

First, we know that pursuits are dangerous. The very nature of a pursuit is that a suspect flees to get away and at least one police vehicle chases to apprehend. The driving behavior creates a varying degree of risk to the public, the officer, and the suspect. We know from our interviews with suspects and other reports that most suspects are "glued" to their rear-view mirrors and are focused on the police car(s) behind them rather than paying sufficient attention to the road ahead. We have learned from analyses of pursuit events that while a few suspects will stop after a chase has started, most will continue to flee until the police terminate the pursuit or they crash.

We also know from interviews with officers and suspects how adrenaline leads active participants in pursuits to make decisions not based on reason or logic, but on emotions and the desire to escape or apprehend, which can cloud the decision-making process. We know that approximately 30 % of reported pursuits result in a crash and that at least one person will die from a pursuit every day. Pursuits can be very expensive in terms of financial and personal losses. They can turn innocent citizens into victims. Further, police officers who think they are doing the right thing by attempting to apprehend a fleeing suspect must live with the death and destruction of a pursuit that they have decided to continue.

Studies have also shown the positive benefits of pursuit driving. In some cases, police can apprehend serious criminals using pursuits. The question is at what cost? Research indicates that many pursuits begin with traffic infractions, not serious or violent crimes. More generally, it is important to consider both the impact of pursuits on crime prevention and law enforcement as well as the management of risk. Many police administrators who ask these questions and examine external research as well as their own data along with legal precedents have responded by restricting policies, enhancing and improving training, requiring active supervision, and developing accountability systems.

Further complicating matters is the current context in which police find themselves—an era of proactivity and innovation, as noted in Chap. 1. Any analysis of a police pursuit must take place within this new context. Today's policing is different from the policing of the 1970s, and there have been many changes that have affected the policing environment. In particular, strategic innovations such as community policing, problem solving, policing people and places, and management innovations (i.e., COMPSTAT) and information technologies (i.e., crime analysis, computerized mapping, information sharing systems, and the automation of tasks and systems) are much more prevalent in policing today than in the past. Demands from the public, government funding sources, those who conduct research on police, and law enforcement leaders are calling for more proactive, focused, place-based, legitimate, intelligence-led, and research-based tactics to *reduce* and *prevent* crime, not just detect or respond to incidents. All of these innovations and expectations not only change the use and meaning of the patrol vehicle, but they also change the nature and consequences of police pursuits. Lum and Fachner (2008) hypothesized that police are placing themselves in places and situations (e.g., "hot spots," "problem locations") that are more likely to result in the discovery of potential wrongdoing or the possibility of individuals fleeing from them. In other words, this new era of policing probably increases the likelihood of encountering a suspect who will flee even though this era is also marked by increased restriction in the use of pursuits.

However, many of these new and proactive strategies also emphasize enhanced data collection and evaluation of interventions to inform and influence officer and supervisor decision making and accountability (Lum 2013; Ratcliffe 2008; Sherman 1998). This push for greater accountability to crime data and also outcome evaluation research is replacing outdated approaches to decision making that relied primarily on historical approaches, tradition, conventional wisdom or common sense, anecdotes, and hunches. The information resulting from research and analysis provides the management team with a new level of knowledge that can help them make informed decisions about policies, training, supervision, and accountability. Specifically, police managers cannot make evidence-based, proactive, intelligence-led, or effective street-level discretionary policy decisions, nor can they hold officers and supervisors accountable, without accurate and timely data.

This new context of policing affects the opportunity structure and risk of engaging in pursuits for police officers. Not only can proactivity informed by information place officers at greater risk to engage in pursuits, but it also requires a greater accounting of the nature, costs, benefits, and consequences of pursuits. It also requires law enforcement to address the fact that pursuit tactics remain unevaluated. The need for more accurate, consistent, and reliable data about the occurrence and characteristics of pursuits, as well as the use of existing knowledge to guide pursuit policy and practice, therefore becomes a *sine qua non* for the use and accountability of this tactic in this new era of policing.

Collecting Better Data, and Nationally

Given what we do know, what do we still need to know? While we have progressed a great deal in our accounting of pursuits, research findings only provide us with knowledge about the nature and characteristics of the *reported* pursuits. We still need a better estimate of the true base rate of pursuits. This number determines how well we can compare costs and benefits of pursuits as well as how often officers violate pursuit policies. For example, "uneventful" pursuits may likely be underreported in many of these databases, causing an overestimation in the proportion of pursuits reported that result in injury or arrest. Police officers may not report or even remember every pursuit. Pursuits that begin in vehicles but that evolve into chases on foot may be underreported. The police may also not report pursuits that do not result in apprehension or that end quickly. Suspected vehicles may voluntarily stop after a short pursuit, leading officers to not conceptualize the incident as a "pursuit."

Only improvements in data collection, analysis, evaluation, and management, combined with motivated leadership, can improve this current situation. The availability, relevance, quality, and content of empirical studies of police pursuits depend on the accurate, timely, and comprehensive collection of data. This includes in-house as well as regional or national incident reporting systems and requirements that can provide an evidentiary base for agencies to tailor such policies to fit their specific needs. If police practices are to become evidence-led, as opposed to anecdotally based, decisions about police pursuit policies must be made using reliable information (Alpert 1988). Fennessy et al. emphasized this goal of better data collection on pursuits early on (1970) and Fennessy and Joscelyn (1972) called for the development of a "hot pursuits" database:

> Without knowledge of the nature of the hot pursuit problem within a jurisdiction it will be impossible to formulate a rational policy or to avoid the misallocation of resources. … we strongly recommend the collection and analysis of a large seasonal sample of data on the incidence, characteristics, and consequences of hot pursuit and the collection and analysis of a representative sample of data on fleeing offenders' characteristics. Careful investigation should also be made of the reasons that underlie the decision to evade arrest and the police officer pursuit motivation" (Fennessy and Joscelyn 1972, p. 400).

As already reviewed, there have been attempts by individual states, such as Minnesota and California, to more systematically collect pursuit data. The International Association of Chiefs of Police (IACP) has also attempted to create a national pursuits database as part of its interest in developing pursuit policy. Indeed, Alpert et al. (1996) described the IACP's creation of its *Vehicular Pursuit Model Policy*[1] as a "significant reform" (pp. I–4) in this area of police managerial policy. In the 1990s, the National Institute of Justice's Office of Science and Technology formed the Pursuit Management Task Force (PMTF) to further examine police pursuits. Among the PMTF's many recommendations,[2] it suggested that law enforcement agencies needed "a national model for collection of pursuit statistics … perhaps through the IACP or similar professional law enforcement organization, for the purpose of encouraging and facilitating research and to expand the body of knowledge relating to pursuits" (Bayless and Osborne 1998: 63).

In response, the IACP, under its *Cutting Edge of Technology Project*,[3] began the Police Pursuit Database Project in 2000. The project's goal was to create an Internet-based, interactive, computerized reporting system by which police agencies could submit and manage reports of vehicular pursuits and, in turn, access the full database for statistical reports compiled from all pursuits recorded in the database. The idea behind a national database was to develop a system in which agencies could gain a shared understanding of pursuit trends across the United States to help guide an agency's future managerial decisions, assessments, policy reforms, and training needs.

Lum and Fachner (2008) provide a detailed description and evaluation of the IACP's national pursuit database. At the time of their writing, only 56 law enforcement agencies were participating in submitting pursuits. This database is now maintained by Pursuits®[4] in cooperation by the IACP and collects the same variables as were collected in the original database.[5] Although the database and full reports are only accessible by those who contribute to the database (login access), the executive summary[6] states that reports have "analyzed more than 1,700 law enforcement pursuits from 2009 and 2010 … more than 1,600 law enforcement pursuits from 2010 and 2011 … more than 2,000 police pursuits from 2011 and 2012." However, these numbers are not too far from earlier yearly averages—approximately 1,530 pursuits from 2003 to 2006—found by Lum and Fachner. It is clear that convincing agencies to participate in the national pursuits database has continued to be a challenge.

---

[1] See http://www.theiacp.org/documents/pdfs/Publications/VehicularPursuitPolicy.pdf.

[2] The full report by Bayless and Osborne (1998) can be downloaded from the National Law Enforcement and Corrections Technology Center (http://www.nlectc.org/pdffiles/pmtf.pdf). Additionally, a Research Review Brief has been published about the report by the National Institute of Justice (see http://www.ncjrs.gov/pdffiles/fs000225.pdf).

[3] See http://www.theiacp.org/research/RCDTechCuttingEdge.html.

[4] See http://www.login4pursuits.net/about.asp.

[5] Compare http://www.login4pursuits.net/Pursuits%20Data%20Form.pdf with page 52, Figure D of Lum and Fachner (2008).

[6] See http://www.login4pursuits.net/2013%20Executive%20Summary.pdf.

Another possible source of data about police pursuits is The Commission on Accreditation for Law Enforcement Agencies, Inc. (CALEA). Agencies that are accredited by CALEA are required to collect and analyze pursuit data. If CALEA would collect and combine these data, it would improve our knowledge about pursuits without a new or extensive data-collection effort.

Despite these efforts, to increase the range of information on pursuits to meet the challenges of pursuits in our age of innovation, better, more, and researcher-accessible data are needed. This effort involves encouraging or mandating the majority of agencies in the United States to collect and evaluate information on all police pursuits, as is done by CALEA. But the quality and culture surrounding the collection of pursuits data and the importance attributed to that collection must begin with individual law enforcement agencies. Police departments, highway patrols, sheriffs, and state law enforcement agencies need to require a report on every pursuit as they should on use of force incidents. The data from these reports must be used to determine if the actions of each officer and supervisor were appropriate and if there are trends or patterns that emerge from the data. One possible approach is to include pursuits in an agency's Early Warning System. This analytical phase is similar to what is expected by accrediting agencies for modifications in management and training as well as personnel actions. While the analysis of their own pursuits will help managers, it is also important for them to know trends in similar agencies throughout their region, state, and the country.

In terms of the depth of data collected, computerizing more information about each individual pursuit within these databases, and doing so with accuracy, must be increased. Commonly collected data on pursuits have included the time of day, reason for pursuit, traffic, road, and environmental conditions, numbers of individuals, vehicles, police cars involved, and speeds, among other risks, and the outcomes of pursuits (injuries, crashes, property damage, criminal charges). However, other types of information may prove useful in not only predicting situations, places, and individuals at high risk for creating a negative outcome (injury, collision, damage, liability), but also in evaluating the effects of pursuit policies and changes in policies. Such information may include:

- Characteristics and history of police officers involved (age, gender, race, time in service, work histories, training)
- Characteristics of fleeing suspects (age, gender, race, socioeconomic status, blood-alcohol levels of drivers, prior criminal histories, driver license histories, drug abuse, etc.)
- Information about vehicles involved in pursuits (types, year, make, and model)
- Knowledge about the places where pursuits occur (e.g., population density, traffic patterns, street layouts, speeding limits, pedestrian information, near misses)
- More information on the decision making criteria used by officers when terminating a pursuit
- Administrative responses to pursuits (see Alpert et al. 1997; Best and Eves 2005)

The analysis of the pursuit should not be limited to the driving or the decisions made by the officer(s) involved. The risk created by the suspect, the factors influencing the pursuit, and all the outcome measures, including costs and benefits, should be part of the analytic scheme. One aspect of pursuit driving about which we know very little is the cost of a pursuit in terms of damage to vehicles, costs of injuries to officers, workers' compensation, emotional stress, and other related costs, including litigation. It is equally important to gauge the impact on community legitimacy. For example, if a violent criminal is apprehended, the community is likely to support the police effort. However, if a prominent member, child, or innocent bystander of the community is injured or killed, the community response may be devastating to the agency and its leadership.

This type of information could facilitate both in-house and comparative analysis and be used to explore research questions such as:

- Do pursuits that take place in urban, population-dense areas tend to result in more bystander injuries than those which do not?
- Do officers who operate on open highways and routes tend to initiate pursuits as a result of routine traffic violations as opposed to those who work within rural areas or inside of cities with lower speed limits?
- Are there relationships between organizational characteristics of police agencies and particular pursuit outcomes or tendencies of an officer to initiate a pursuit?
- What are the characteristics of suspects, officers, or communities that increase or decrease the risk of pursuits and/or negative outcomes?
- What characteristics of pursuits themselves tend to lead to more negative outcomes?
- What is the impact of changes in pursuit policy on agency legitimacy with the community?
- What are the impact of media and other video coverage of pursuits on their frequency as well as public perceptions?

Evaluating Pursuit Tactics

Even if police agencies are collecting better data on pursuits, policies and practices may not be regularly informed by that data or research (Alpert et al. 2000, p. 15). It is also important to continue our efforts to understand the impact of the use of pursuits and also pursuit policy changes on policing, the officers, crime, and citizens. Important questions that remain unanswered are, for example:

- Does a change in the type of pursuit policy (for example, from a more judgmental to a more restrictive policy) lead to a reduction of negative outcomes, lawsuits, or damage costs?
- Are different types of technologies to stop fleeing vehicles effective and cost-effective?
- Do changes in pursuit policies affect the crime in a given jurisdiction?
- Do changes in pursuit policies affect the outcomes of a pursuit?
- Can costs and benefits of pursuits be calculated correctly and do communities have certain thresholds of the cost–benefit ratios (irrespective of legal precedents)?

Data that shed light on these and other questions can help agencies make better choices about the types of policies they adopt and when they should pursue fleeing suspects. For example, there is a debate about the impact of not chasing fleeing suspects. Agencies may believe that by not chasing cars, they may be encouraging suspects to flee from traffic and enforcement stops. While the data from the Orlando, Florida, Police Department refutes those claims and shows that citizens who flee are not impacted by a change on policy, we need to learn more about the impact of a change in policy and practice (see discussion in Alpert et al. 2006). Unfortunately, we do not have information from multiple agencies to compare suspect behavior before and after a change in policy or practice. While suspects may be arrested for more serious crimes, we must distinguish between what the police know that influences their decision to continue a chase, what occurs during the chase, and what is learned during and after the pursuit. Clearly, data show that the most frequent act known to the police as a pursuit begins is a traffic infraction or other minor offense.

Unfortunately, we do not know the impact of increased penalties for fleeing and eluding the police. Many have suggested that fleeing drivers should face serious penalties when apprehended, and different states have varying "legal" responses to fleeing. Regrettably, we do not have data on the impact of different policies and practices and do not know if implementing swift and sure punishment would encourage suspects to drive more dangerously or give up and stop more frequently. We do know that prosecuting attorneys often drop charges of fleeing and eluding during plea bargaining, to the dismay of victims and their families. Restricting pursuits by policy is one way of reducing the frequency of chases, but it may be that the percentage or ratio of pursuits to crashes and even injuries is not impacted by such a change. We need to define universally what is a pursuit as well as the relevant information to record.

Yet another reason for more data in today's policing context is the advent of new information and tactical technologies related to pursuits. Police now have mobile computer terminals, instant access to motor vehicle data, and more frequently, license plate readers attached to their vehicles (Lum et al. 2011). All of these information technologies allow officers to know much more about a vehicle and its owners (and possibly occupants). This could include whether the individual has any open warrants or a history of violence. In the past, police could only guess who might be in the vehicle or the background of the vehicle and its owner. Such information changes the game in terms of the cost–benefit calculation of a pursuit.

Law enforcement also has used other pursuing vehicles, such as helicopters. Alpert (1998a) has found that when helicopters pursue vehicles, apprehension can occur without a crash. Of course, determining whether pursuits are worthwhile to begin with, especially given the high cost of using air support resources, also requires more data. Other types of technologies in need of evaluation might also include the use of GPS systems that track stolen vehicles. For example, one new technology known as StarChase[7] is a device designed to tag and track a vehicle that

---

[7] See http://www.starchase.com/.

flees from the police. It involves firing a projectile with a GPS unit attached into a pursuing vehicle. An initial assessment of StarChase by Alpert (2013) shows promise for the use of technology to reduce the dangers of pursuits. As one officer from the Arizona Department of Public Safety noted, such technologies can be a "game changer" for law enforcement. While there are selection, training and accountability issues that need to be resolved, the results of successful applications of StarChase to date are impressive. Drivers of vehicles that are tagged behave as if they are free from the police and slow down when the police stop chasing, in many cases within a relatively short time and distance. The behavior of the fleeing suspects demonstrates that they have no knowledge that they are being tracked by a GPS system that pinpoints their location and speed in real time. This finding is also consistent with prior research of offenders (see Dunham et al., 1998). In most cases, officers have tactically apprehended suspects and seized vehicles and contraband without creating a risk to the public, themselves or the suspect or any passengers. We advocate any tagging and tracking technology that can reduce pursuits, and are impressed with the findings from the preliminary analysis of StarChase, but suggest that any new technology must be evaluated for costs and benefits as well as effectiveness.

Evaluating existing technologies can help us better understanding whether such technologies are either outdated given the more restrictive pursuit policies that appear to be the current trend, or are ineffective in reducing or stopping fleeing felons. The IACP pursuits database mentions at least five stopping technologies: PIT maneuvers, roadblocks, rolling roadblocks, tire deflators, and engine disablers. We have yet to find an evaluation of whether each of these, compared to other options, leads to "successful" outcomes of pursuits (however defined).

Overall, the themes of these recommendations emphasize the reporting of all pursuits, an increase and refinement of data on pursuit and pursuit-related activities, and the use of those data for purposes of evaluation of pursuit technologies. The need to use meaningful data and analytic techniques to evaluate and manage pursuits is especially important in an age of policing that encourages both the use of proactive and evidence-based tactics to reduce crime, and also increased legitimacy and accountability. This also means that lawyers and courts must pay more attention to research in their decisions, and police managers must use pursuit data to understand more thoroughly the factors that increase the risk and prevalence of negative outcomes. Conversely, managers must use these data to understand the acceptable limits of pursuits. In other words, while the negative decisions must be reduced, the positive facets of pursuits must be defined and accepted. In hopes of translating pursuits research into daily police practice, all of these efforts need improvement to advance this important policy arena.

References

42 U.S.C. §1983.
42 U.S.C. §1988.
Allen v. City of West Memphis, No. 11–5266, (6th Cir., filed October 9 2012).
Brower v. Inyo County, 489 U.S. 593 (1989).
Chambers v. Ideal Pure Milk Co., 245 S.W.2d 589 (1952).
County of Sacramento v. Lewis, 523 U.S. 833 (1998).
Graham v. Connor, 490 U.S. 386, 388 (1989).
Lytle v. Bexar County, 560 F.3d 404, 414 (5th Cir. 2009).
Monell v. Department of Social Services of New York, 436 U.S. 658 (1978).
Monroe v. Pape, 365 U.S. 167 (1961).
Scott v. Harris, 550 U.S. 372 (2007).
Smith v. Cupp, 430 F.3d 766, 776–77 (6th Cir. 2005).
Swindle v. City of Memphis, No. CT-005342-09, (Div. IX).
Sykes v. United States, 131 S. Ct. 2267 (2011).
Tennessee v. Garner, 471 U.S. 1 (1985).
United States Constitution, Amendment IV.
United States Constitution, Amendment XIV.
Walker v. Davis, 649 F. 3d 502 (6th Cir. 2011).
Whren v. United States, 517 U.S. 806 (1996).

Alpert, G.P. 1987. Questioning police pursuits in urban areas. *Journal of Police Science and Administration, 15(4)*, 298–306.
Alpert, G.P. 1988. Police Pursuit: Linking Data to Decisions. *Criminal Law Bulletin, 24*, 453–462.
Alpert, G. 1997. Police Pursuit: Policies and Training. *National Institute of Justice, Research in Brief.* Washington, DC: National Institute of Justice.
Alpert, G.P. 1998a. *Helicopters in pursuit operations.* Washington, DC: National Institute of Justice.
Alpert, G.P. 1998b. A factorial analysis of police pursuit Driving Decisions. *Justice Quarterly 15*, 347–359.
Alpert, G.P. 2013. *StarChase: Draft Report.* Draft report submitted to the National Institute of Justice.
Alpert, G.P. and Anderson, P.R. 1986. The most deadly force: Police pursuits. *Justice Quarterly, 3(1)*, 1–14.
Alpert, G.P. and Dunham, R.G. 1988. Research on police pursuits: Applications for law enforcement. *American Journal of Police, 7(2)*, 123–133.
Alpert, G.P. and Dunham, R.G. 1989. Policing hot pursuits: The discovery of aleatory elements. *Journal of Criminal Law and Criminology, 80(2)*, 521–539.

G.P. Alpert and C. Lum, *Police Pursuit Driving: Policy and Research*, SpringerBriefs in Criminology, DOI 10.1007/978-1-4939-0712-0, © The Author(s) 2014

Alpert, G.P. and Dunham, R.G. 1990. *Police pursuit driving: Controlling responses to emergency situations.* Westport, CT: Greenwood Press.

Alpert, G.P. and Fridell, L. 1992. *Police vehicle and firearms: Instruments of deadly force.* Prospect Heights, IL: Waveland.

Alpert, G.P., Kenney, D.J., and Dunham, R.G. 1997. Police pursuits and the use of force: Recognizing and managing "the pucker factor" – a research note. *Justice Quarterly, 14(2),* 371–385.

Alpert, G., Kenney, D., Dunham, R., and Smith, W. 2000. *Police pursuits: What we know.* Washington, DC: Police Executive Research Forum.

Alpert, G., R. Dunham, and M. Stroshine. 2006. *Policing: Continuity and Change.* Prospect Heights, IL: Waveland Press.

Alpert. G.P., Kenney, D.J., Dunham, R.G.., Smith, W., and Cosgrove, M. 1996. *Police pursuit and the use of force.* Final report to the National Institute of Justice: Washington, DC.

Alpert, G. and Smith, W. 2008. Police pursuits after *Scott v. Harris*: Far from ideal? *Ideas in American Policing Paper Series.* Washington, DC: Police Foundation.

American Civil Liberties Union Foundation of Southern California. 1996. *Not just isolated incidents: The epidemic of police pursuits in southern California.* Los Angeles, CA: American Civil Liberties Union Foundation of Southern California.

Australian Institute of Criminology. 2013. Motor vehicle pursuit-related fatalities in Australia 2000–11. *Trends and Issues in Crime and Criminal Justice, 452.*

Auten, J. 1991. *Police pursuit driving operations in Illinois: 1990.* Champaign, IL: Police Training Institute, University of Illinois.

Barton, G. 2013. Police chief credits new policy for drop in high-speed chases. *Journal Sentinel* (September 7, 2013). http://www.jsonline.com/news/crime/police-chief-credits-new-policy-for-drop-in-high-speed-chases-b9992566z1-222824431.html (downloaded 9/8/2013).

Bayless, K. and Osborne, R. 1998. *Pursuit management task force report.* Washington, D.C.: National Law Enforcement and Corrections Technology Center for the National Institute of Justice.

Beckman, E. 1985. *A report to law enforcement on factors in police pursuits.* East Lansing, MI: School of Criminal Justice, Michigan State University.

Best, D. and Eves, K. 2004. *Police pursuits in Wales:* The *results from a one-year monitoring exercise in the four Welsh police forces 2002–2003.* Wales, UK: Police Complaints Authority.

Best, D. and Eves, K. 2005. *Why are there no lessons learned from road traffic incidents involving the police?* Wales, UK: Police Complaints Authority.

Braga, A., Weisburd, D., Waring, E., Green-Mazerolle, L., Spelman, W., and Gajewski, F. 1999. Problem-oriented policing in violent crime places: A randomized controlled experiment. *Criminology, 37,* 541–580.

Brewer, N. and McGrath, G. 1991. Characteristics of offenders in high-speed pursuits. *American Journal of Police, 10(3),* 63–68.

California Highway Patrol. 1983. *California Highway Patrol pursuit study.* Sacramento, CA: California Highway Patrol.

California Highway Patrol. 2011. *Report to the Legislature, Senate Bill 719, police pursuits.* Available at: www.chp.ca.gov/html/pdf/police_pursuit_report_2011.pdf.

Carlan, P. 2006. Professionalism. In J. Greene (Ed.) *Police encyclopedia, 3rd Edition.* New York, NY: Routledge.

Charles, M.T., Falcone, D.N., and Wells, E. 1992. *Police pursuit in pursuit of policy: The pursuit issue, legal and literature review, and an empirical study.* Washington, DC: AAA Foundation for Traffic Safety.

Crew, R. 1992. An effective strategy for hot pursuit: Some evidence from Houston. *American Journal of Police, 11(3),* 89–95.

Crew, R. and Hart, R.A., Jr. 1999. Assessing the value of police pursuit. *Policing: An International Journal of Police Strategies and Management, 22(1),* 58–73.

Crime and Misconduct Commission. 2011. *An alternative to pursuits: A review of the evade police provisions.* Fortitude Valley, Australia: Crime and Misconduct Commission, Queensland.

Criminal Justice Commission. 1998. *Police pursuits in Queensland resulting in death or injury*. Brisbane, Queensland: Criminal Justice Commission.

Cullen, F., Myer, A., and Latessa, E. 2009. Eight Lessons from *Moneyball*: The high cost of ignoring evidence-based corrections. *Victims and Offenders, 4*, 197–213.

Docking, M., Bucke, T., Grace, K., and Dady, H. 2007. *Police road traffic incidents: A study of cases involving serious and fatal injuries*. London, U.K.: Independent Police Complaints Commission.

Dunham, R.G. and Alpert, G.P. 1991. Understanding the dynamics of officer age and gender in police pursuits. *American Journal of Police, 10(3)*, 51–62.

Dunham, R.G., Alpert, G.P., Kenney, D.J., and Cromwell, P. 1998. High-speed pursuits: The offenders' perspective. *Criminal Justice and Behavior, 25*, 30–45.

Falcone, D., Wells, E., and Charles, M. 1992. *Police pursuit in pursuit of policy: The empirical study, Volume II*. Washington, DC: AAA Foundation for Traffic Safety.

Fennessy, E.F., Hamilton, T., Joscelyn, K.B., and Merrit, J.S. 1970. *A study of the problem of hot pursuit*. Washington, DC: U.S. Department of Transportation.

Fennessy, E.F. and Joscelyn, K.B. 1972. A national study of hot pursuit. *Denver University Law Journal, 48*, 389–403.

Hannigan, M.J. 1995. *The evaluation of risk: Initial cause vs. final outcome in police pursuits*. Sacramento, CA: California Highway Patrol.

Hicks, W.L. 2006. Police vehicular pursuits: A descriptive analysis of state agencies' written policies. *Policing: An International Journal of Police Strategies and Management, 29(1)*, 106–124.

Hoffman, G. 2003. *Police pursuits: A law enforcement and public safety issue for Queensland*. Brisbane, Queensland: Queensland Crime and Misconduct Commission.

Homel, R. 1990. *High speed police pursuits in Perth: A report to the Police Department of Western Australia*. Perth, Western Australia: Department of Western Australia.

Hutson, H.R., Rice, P., Chana, J.K., Kyriacou, D.N., Chang, Y., and Miller, R.M. 2007. A review of police pursuit fatalities in the United States from 1982–2004. *Prehospital Emergency Care, 11*, 278–283.

Jang, H., Lee, C.-B., and Hoover, L.T. 2012. Dallas' disruption unit: Efficacy of hot spots deployment. *Policing: An International Journal of Police Strategies and Management, 35(3)*, 593–614.

Josi D.A., Donahue M.E., and Magnus, R. 2000. Conducting blue light specials or drilling holes in the sky: Are increased traffic stops better than routine patrol in taking a bite out of crime? *Police Practice and Research, 1*, 477–507.

Kelling, G. and Moore, M. 1988. The evolving strategy of policing. *Perspectives on Policing, 4*, 1–15. Washington, DC: National Institute of Justice.

Kenney, D. and Alpert, G. 1997. A national survey of pursuits and the use of police force: Data from law enforcement agencies. *Journal of Criminal Justice, 25(4)*, 315–323.

Koper, C. and Mayo-Wilson, E. 2006. Police crackdowns for illegal gun carrying: A systematic review of their impacts on gun crimes. *Journal of Experimental Criminology, 2(2)*, 227–261.

Lawler, J. 2013. *Analysis of the 2012 Milwaukee Police Department Vehicle Pursuits*. Milwaukee, MN: Milwaukee Police Department.

Lucadamo, T. 1994. *Identifying the dimension of police pursuit*. Master's Thesis, University of Maryland.

Lum, C. 2009. Translating police research into practice. *Ideas in American Policing*. Washington, DC: Police Foundation.

Lum, C. 2013. Is crime analysis evidence-based? *Translational Criminology Magazine*. Fairfax, VA: George Mason University, Center for Evidence-Based Crime Policy.

Lum, C. and Fachner, G. 2008. *Police pursuits in an age of innovation and reform*. Alexandria, VA: International Association of Chiefs of Police.

Lum, Cynthia and Christopher Koper. 2013. Evidence-Based Policing. In G. Bruinsma and D. Weisburd (Eds.), *The Encyclopedia of Criminology and Criminal Justice*, pp. 1426–1437. New York: Springer-Verlag.

Lum, C., Hibdon, J., Cave, B., Koper C., and Merola, L. 2011. License plate reader (LPR) police patrols in crime hot spots: An experimental evaluation in two adjacent jurisdictions. *Journal of Experimental Criminology 7(4)*, 321–345.

Lum, C., Koper, C., and Telep, C. 2011 [published online 2010]). The evidence-based policing matrix. *Journal of Experimental Criminology* 7(1), 3–26.

Lum, C., Telep, C., Koper, C.S., and Grieco J. 2012. Receptivity to Research in Policing. *Justice Policy and Research 14(1):* 61–95.

Madden, T. and Alpert, G. 1999. Toward the development of a pursuit decision calculus: Pursuit benefits versus pursuit cost. *Justice Research and Policy 1,* 23–41.

McGarrell E.F., Chermak, S., and Weiss, A. 2002. Reducing gun violence: Evaluation of the Indianapolis Police Department's directed patrol project. Washington, DC: National Institute of Justice.

McGarrell, E.F., Chermak, S., Weiss, A., and Wilson, J. 2001. Reducing firearms violence through directed police patrol. *Criminology and Public Policy 1,* 119–148.

Moore, M. 1992. Problem solving and community policing: A preliminary assessment of new strategies of policing. In N. Morris and M. Tonry (Eds.), *Modern policing. Crime and Justice, Vol. 15.* Chicago, IL: University of Chicago Press.

National Research Council. 2004. *Fairness and effectiveness in policing: The evidence.* (W. Skogan and K. Frydl, Eds.). Washington, DC: National Academies Press.

Nelson, D. and Brune, T. 1991, June 30. In hot pursuit: One-third of police chases end in crashes--and some elude rules. *Chicago Sun Times,* 1, 18.

Nichols, L.J. 2004. *Managing police pursuits: Findings from IACP's police pursuit database.* Alexandria, VA: International Association of Chiefs of Police.

Nugent, H. Connors, E., McEwen, T., and Mayo, L. 1990. *Restrictive policies for high-speed police pursuits.* Washington, DC: U.S. Department of Justice, National Institute of Justice, Office of Communication and Research Utilization.

Oechsli, S. 1992. *Kentucky State police pursuit study: 1989–1992.* Frankfort, KY: Kentucky State Police.

O'Keefe, J.L., Jr. 1989. An empirical analysis of high speed police pursuits: The Houston Police Department experience. Ann Arbor, MI: University of Michigan Microfilms International.

Patinkin, H. and Bingham, K. 1986. Police motor vehicle pursuits: The Chicago experience. *The Police Chief, 55,* 61–62.

Payne, D.M. and Fenske, J.C. 1997. An analysis of the rates of accidents, injuries and fatalities under different light conditions: A Michigan emergency response study of state police pursuits. *Policing: An International Journal of Police Strategies and Management, 20(2),* 357–373.

Physicians for Automotive Safety. 1968. *Rapid pursuit by police. Causes, hazards, and consequences: A national pattern is evident.* New York, NY: Physicians for Automotive Safety.

Ratcliffe, J. 2008. *Intelligence-led policing.* Portland, OR: Willan Publishing.

Reiss, A. 1992. Police organization in the twentieth century. In N. Morris and M. Tonry (Eds.) *Modern Policing. Crime and Justice, Vol. 15.* Chicago, IL: University of Chicago Press.

Rivara, F. P. and Mack, C. D. 2004. Motor vehicle crash deaths related to police pursuits in the United States. *Injury Prevention, 10(2),* 93–95.

Schultz, D., E. Hudak and G. Alpert. 2009. Emergency Driving and Pursuits: The Officer's Perspective. FBI Law Enforcement Bulletin 78: 1–7.

Senese, J.D. and Lucadamo, T. 1996. To pursue or not to pursue? That is the question: Modeling police vehicular pursuits. *American Journal of Police, XV(4),* 55–77.

Sharp, A. 2003. The dynamic of vehicle chases in real life. *Law and Order,* 68–74.

Sherman, L. 1990. Police Crackdowns: Initial and Residual Deterrence. *Crime and Justice: A Review of Research* Volume *12,* 1–48.

Sherman, L. 1998. Evidence-based policing. *Ideas in American Policing Paper Series.* Washington, DC: Police Foundation.

Sherman, L. and Eck, J. 2002. Policing for Crime Prevention. In Sherman, L., Farrington, D., Welsh, B., and MacKenzie, D. (Eds.). *Evidence based crime prevention.* London, UK: Routledge.

Sherman, L., Farrington, D., Welsh, B., and MacKenzie, D. (Eds.). 2002. *Evidence based crime prevention.* London, UK: Routledge.

Sherman, L., Gottfredson, D.C., MacKenzie, D.L., Eck, J.E., Reuter, P.H., and Bushway, S.D. 1997. *Preventing crime: What works, what doesn't, what's promising.* Washington, DC: National Institute of Justice.

Sherman, L., Shaw, J., and Rogan, D. 1995. *The Kansas City gun experiment* (Research in Brief). Washington, DC: National Institute of Justice.

Sherman, L. and Weisburd, D. 1995. General deterrent effects of police patrol in crime hot spots: A randomized controlled trial. *Justice Quarterly 12,* 625–648.

Taylor, B., Koper, C. S., and Woods, D. J. 2011. A randomized controlled trial of different policing strategies at hot spots of violent crime. *Journal of Experimental Criminology, 7,* 149–181.

U.S. Department of Justice, Bureau of Justice Statistics. 2006. *Law enforcement management and administrative statistics (LEMAS): 2003 sample survey of law enforcement agencies.* ICPSR version. Washington, DC: U.S. Dept. of Commerce, Bureau of the Census. Ann Arbor, MI: Inter-university Consortium for Political and Social Research.

U.S. Department of Justice, Bureau of Justice Statistics. 2007. *Census of state and local law enforcement agencies 2004.* (Bulletin authored by Brian Reaves). Retrieved February 1 2008 from http://www.ojp.usdoj.gov/bjs/abstract/csllea04.htm.

Victoria Police Service. 2012. *Inspectorate review 20/2011. Evaluation of Pursuits: Final Report.* Victoria, Australia.

Weisburd, D. and Braga, A. (Eds.). 2006. *Policing innovation: Contrasting perspectives.* Cambridge, UK: Cambridge University Press.

Weisburd, D. and Eck, J. 2004. What can police do to reduce crime, disorder, and fear? *Annals of the American Academy of Political and Social Science, 593,* 42–65.

Weiss, A. and McGarrell, E.F. 1996, November. *The impact of increased traffic enforcement on crime.* Paper presented to the American Society of Criminology, Chicago.

Wells, E., and Falcone, D.N. 1997. Research on police pursuits: Advantages of multiple data collection strategies. *Policing: An International Journal of Police Strategies and Management, 20*(4), 729–748.

Index

G.P. Alpert and C. Lum, *Police Pursuit Driving: Policy and Research*, SpringerBriefs
in Criminology, DOI 10.1007/978-1-4939-0712-0, © The Author(s) 2014

Made in the USA
Columbia, SC
16 January 2019